Pain & Paradox
The Path of Praise
A Personal Journey

Sandi McReynolds

ISBN-13:
978-1484901991

ISBN-10:
1484901991

DEDICATION

For any who struggle with pain and confusion along this often-dark path of praise.

For Mac, my partner in this wouldn't-trade-it-for anything journey.

And most of all for Jesus, the Name that <u>must</u> be praised.

.

FORWARD

I have known the author for over 20 years as pastor, friend and co-worker in the Kingdom. In my own way I have had at least a second row seat in the journey she so honestly takes you on in this story of the faithful love of God. Rarely, have I read someone who is willing to tell it as it is when it comes to the "problem of pain" as C.S. Lewis would put it. I found myself agreeing on a level that was more than intellectual. She put into words the place we find ourselves in our hearts with God when we suffer with Him. I recommend her story, in many ways it's your story too. It will encourage your heart and the heart of those you know who find themselves in the place we don't understand called trouble.

Jay St. Clair
Community Outreach Minister
College Heights Christian Church
Joplin, Missouri

CONTENTS

Dedication

Forward

Contents

Acknowledgments

Prologue

Chapter 1 1
on Pain & Paradox

Chapter 2 11
of ADHDogs

Chapter 3 19
on Healing Hearts

Chapter 4 24
of Hands that Build

Chapter 5 29
ADHDogs and Scooter

Chapter 6 32
Sweet Memories & Hard Truths

Chapter 7 35
Manna Every Morning

Chapter 8..43
the Problem of Scooter

Chapter 9..45
More Paths to the Bridge

Chapter 10..48
of Purpose-Driven Pain

Chapter 11 49
His Presence in the Wilderness

Chapter 12..55
the Bridge ˜from a Ruined City

Chapter 13..56
Principalities and Powers

Chapter 14..58
of God-whispers in the Chaos

Chapter 15..62
Pursuing Happiness & Planting Joy

Chapter 16..65
of Elephants in the Garden

Chapter 17 69
A Riddle

Chapter 18..83
Finding Hope

ACKNOWLEDGMENTS

Cover by Ryan McCoy, Shortleaf Photography
Lessons by Spanky and Scooter—and Father God

"For I know the plans I have for you," declares the LORD, "plans to prosper you and not to harm you, plans to give you hope and a future. Then you will call on me and come and pray to me, and I will listen to you."
Jeremiah 29:11-12

Prologue
The Journey

SEVERAL YEARS AGO, I found myself on a journey that ultimately became the hardest of my life. I certainly didn't expect it to be. I am still surprised at the intensity of it. I would like to think that if I had known then what I know now, I would have begun the trip anyway, but to be honest, I have asked my merciful God more than once why He didn't just let me stay where I was; perfectly happy spending time with my family and working in my garden, "doing good deeds," and volunteering in my favorite ministries and projects.

My motives were good when I took the first step. My intentions were even better when subsequent steps became more and more painful and confusing.

I have never been more certain it was His idea. His call was clear—He had been preparing and equipping me my whole life for this purpose.

I doubt I will ever really understand all the "why's" that haunt my heart. I look forward to the day I can truly, genuinely lay every one on the altar before my God as a sacrifice of praise. In the meantime, I know He is using every pain and paradox to teach (and re-teach) lessons I might not learn any other way.

These pages are compilations of my journal. My effort to understand and articulate those lessons, undeniably *self*-focused and *self*ishly cathartic. But my Father always has a good plan. He will use even the *self* stuff to bless others—and us. I am grateful.

It is an evolving journey, far from over. There is still so much to learn. I know that on THAT DAY every paradox will become blessing and every pain turn to joy—fitting sacrifice to lay at His feet. But the journey is *now*, and His promise of *then* still shines through a glass that is dark. The path still leads through hard and dangerous places. I still struggle to trust the hand I cannot see.

Clearly, one of the next steps in my journey is to share what He is teaching me, in whatever way He leads. This paradox is reassuring—and humbling: He really is strongest in my weakness. But His decree is daunting. I really am required to "hang out" my weakness for all to see. He calls me to offer "risky transparency" in ways that sometimes surprise and always challenge. Sometimes it is to simply trust Him, humble myself, and take the risk. Sometimes it is a "just-because" enigma. Sometimes it is obvious He wants to use it to bless another. And sometimes I find He just wants to bless me! (God save me from the times I try to bless myself...)

His good plan is to use every pain and paradox of our lives to lead us along the path of praise He has marked out for us; and He will use the most unlikely of teachers to finally bring us to our bright and shining bridge—His presence and sufficiency.

Chapter 1
on Pain & Paradox...

NOTHING IS EVER WASTED in God's economy—especially pain. Just as He numbers the hairs of our head, He numbers every heart-ache, injury, and injustice; and He will never allow one more than is necessary for His purpose, and our good. He warns me my journey cannot be measured by someone else's experience, or opinion. He numbers my days, and restores my soul when He has accomplished what He wills in it.

(It is painful and overwhelming.)

He cautions there is no shortcut through the grief and pain of loss. If I do not face it and walk through it, it will haunt me until I do, or destroy me if I do not. I can only walk through it one step, one tear at a time, as God leads and empowers. I know He shares my pain and grieves my loss.

(It still hurts and overwhelms.)

He tells me I may never understand why He allows this present agony of spirit, but He promises His plan for me is good, to give me hope and a future.

(It is hard to hold a future hope when pain is so now.)

I have known His "peace that passes understanding" and long for it again. I know the moment I fully trust Him with all my heart, mind and spirit, and want His will more than my own, He will bless me with "joy unspeakable and full of glory!" So why not just do it and save myself a lot of grief? Not a clue! Only He knows what it takes to make me look like Jesus, and ultimately I will be so glad He refused to cut short this time of refining. In the meantime, there are days when the dark is so deep I cannot catch my breath and can only hang on by my fingernails; and other days when every snowflake brings me joy and I relish the privilege of learning all He has to teach me.

God gave me Spanky, my little ADHDog, to make me smile when the darkness closes in—and to show me how much like Spanky His ADHDaughter is, running in circles and whining to reach the big dogs outside where it is cold and stormy, when all the time He is inviting us to play right here where it is warm and cozy.

Spanky helps me understand——just a little—how God can love a stubborn, troublesome, hapless critter simply because He chose it and it is His; even when it hits the wall chasing a toy or gets into forbidden "stuff," or gives the most affection to him who has the treat.

A "short leash" is a wonderful tool to teach Spanky obedience and submission.

And me...

God is the God of order and reason. He calls me to seek His face and follow and obey Him. He smiles when I trust Him before I understand His reasons. But He is never unreasoning.

People are often chaotic and illogical. His compassion and mercy are dishonored if we choose to sacrifice someone else and justify it as mandated by God. Silent witnesses who look the other way and walk on by are just as complicit in the injustice. He calls us to be His living sacrifice, but to be sacrificed on the altar of expediency—especially by a brother or sister—is the most miserable of deaths. He calls me to die in humility and courage anyway.

He commands me to be transparent and vulnerable, "harmless as a dove..." *Transparent and vulnerable* is dangerous. It is pretty certain someone will betray my trust, or re-context and violate my confidence and break my heart. He demands transparency anyway.

Being re-formed is hard work. The potter's wheel makes me dizzy and I want to get off. The kiln is blistering and I am sure the gauge must be broken. The curing process is long and my get-it-done spirit protests.

But the hardest work of all is forgiveness.

I am devastated that brothers and sisters I thought were friends were willing to see me wounded and walk away; that those I trusted and confided in most actually participated in, or at least "held the coats" for, the stoning. Good intentions injure and kill as relentlessly as bad, and they are even more hurtful. God demands I forgive. That is hard.

I dread these waves of despair and humiliation. I hate it that I feel sorry for myself. I am angry that I lie naked and bleeding in the ditch, wounded by hands I believe should have defended and lifted me up. I am appalled at how much I care that they walk on the other side of the road so they do not have to see the blood and gore. God demands I forgive unconditionally. That is harder.

I will wound my brother if I ascribe motive based on outcomes. I struggle to avoid it, especially when I learn they unfairly ascribe motive to me. God demands I not only forgive unconditionally, but love unconditionally. That is just too, too hard.

I know that if I refuse to forgive, I choose an "acid that destroys its container;" a "body of death" that will slowly rot and destroy me. If I choose unforgiveness, I am choosing bondage to those who hurt me. I know I will be free of this pain only when I forgive.

Jesus leaves me no options. He says I must forgive to be forgiven. He tells me to return blessing for injury. He commands me to pursue peace, and above all love deeply. But I want to remind Him He said, "...love each other...!" Then He asks, "...where were you when I laid the earth's foundations!?" and my heart breaks; but this time my stubborn will does, too, and I find myself enfolded in His arms and hear Him promise He will rescue me from this body of death.

Thanks be to God, through Jesus Christ our Lord!

Nothing is ever wasted in God's economy. He strikes the match and fans the passion; then calls, prepares and equips. He will complete the work He began in me. He warns me that though He makes my calling sure, He permits me to lay only my own calling before Him, not judge, or be judged by, others. He calls me to pursue peace.

I know, as martyred American missionary Jim Elliot famously said, "He is no fool who gives what he cannot keep to gain what he cannot lose." I can trust that His plan is bigger than I could devise—better than I can imagine. But I cannot embrace a bigger, better plan until I am willing to lay all my hopes and dreams and dearest treasures on His altar and stand before Him empty-handed.

Relinquishment hurts.

When I finally resolve to offer my treasure—my life's work—as a sacrifice of praise and ask Him for help to turn loose, He gently pries my fingers off one by one and tenderly kisses each fingertip. Then He tells me I cannot embrace the bigger, better love He has for me until I let Him do the same thing with my heart.

Brokenness hurts.

My Father promises He saves all my tears in a bottle. Someday soon I will receive them from His very hand. I think those tears will be diamonds and that bottle a crystal vial—beautiful beyond description—but much smaller than it seems in this "dark night of the soul."

Satan's plan is to wear me down, bit by bit. God's plan is to build me up, rule upon rule, precept upon precept. He promises me a good plan, hope and a future, where His rules and precepts bring "glory to glory." But the pit is dark and deep. The loneliness is suffocating. The silence is deafening. If King David and the Prophet Jeremiah—men after God's own heart— dreaded the pit and cried out for rescue, why should I be surprised that my cry is so desperate?

His plan is good. When desperation drives me to at last truly seek Him with all my heart, I feel His gentle presence. He has been here all along, perfecting that which concerns me, *rejoicing over me.*

But He leaves me in the pit! I cry, "How long, Lord? I'll die in this darkness!" And I hear Him chuckle, "That is My good plan! You will die...so you can live. This pit you hate is fertile soil and coming spring. If I shorten the time it takes you to put down new roots, they will be too weak to hold you, or wither and die." So finally I surrender and embrace the dark, and as I burrow deep into its rich softness His fragrance surrounds me. It is then, in the stillness, I hear The Gardener whisper my name: "Now I can teach you to *rejoice with Me.*"

And as He teaches and we rejoice, I learn He not only *rejoices* over me, He *sings* over me. The Creator of the Universe rejoices and sings—over me! I cannot grasp it... until I remember Spanky, and how joyfully I play endless tug-of-war, and love to pet him as he curls in my lap, and tell him "Good boy!" when he gets me up at 4:00 a.m. to go outside...

Then, unbelievable privilege! This Maker and Sustainer of All Things invites me to *sing with Him.* (But why should I wonder that the God of Forever deigns to sing with me, when He gave His Perfect Son to abide with me—forever!) My pit of despair is suddenly a concert hall. He transforms my wavering little notes into soaring harmony and smiles at my delight in His song.

I want this song to last forever. But instead, the Author and Perfecter of my faith gives me a new song—a more complex score than ever—and patiently leads me through practice after practice until I get it right.

He gives me a new voice, and tells me that He made my song to share. He tells me that my song needs other voices, and harmony needs other notes to blend, and it's OK to wish for some "with skin on." The Body is the place He'll make me whole.

The Singer sings my new song with me and all of Heaven hums along. He leads my singing to bless others, and then He smiles His blessing onto me. So I sing my song for the Audience of One, and He makes me a trophy of His grace.

I know that I will see the goodness of the Lord in the land of the living.

God has been trying to teach me the blessings of pain and brokenness—that HE really is enough—since the beginning of this journey, but it took His "short leash" to bring me face to face with ME.

It wasn't a pretty picture—this ADHDaughter running in circles, bumping into walls chasing "toys" Satan throws. I'm so grateful God never gives up, even when I shut my eyes real tight, put my paws over my ears, and bark <u>real loud</u> to drown out what I don't want to hear. His leash is woven grace and mercy, and as it draws me to Him, I finally have no choice but to face my truth.

The truth is, I ran in terror of the silence and loneliness of loss, and even more in fear He would tell me "no" to what I want. The truth is, somewhere along the way I let something besides my God become the center of my life. No wonder my Lovingly Jealous Father had to let it be stripped away! I'm so thankful He is long-suffering and merciful, and loves me enough to do whatever it takes to bring me into right relationship with Him. It has been a long, painful battle, with surely more to come. I'm so glad He always wins.

I know the God of all grace, Who called me to His eternal glory in Christ, after I have suffered a little while, will Himself restore me and make me strong, firm and steadfast. (I Peter 5:10)

God's thoughts are not my thoughts, and often His ways are past finding out. It is clear my Father wants relationships restored, and I long for closure and healing of memories. But it is also clear, and confusing, that His timing is seldom mine. Each time I think I am ready to face this next huge hurdle and risk reaching out to "friends" I feel betrayed me, I am faced with another family crisis—more pain and loss—instead!

My always-healthy, always-strong-when-I-am-weak husband faces yet another surgery—the second in less than a year! Nothing life-threatening as surgeries go, but still a reminder to both of us how tenuous this life really is... and how vulnerable, when post-surgery exams reveal a threat to his transplanted cornea that could require a third, more critical surgery. It is no accident that this "chance" discovery allows doctors to intervene in time to save his eye. We know it is a gift from our Ever-Present Protector, and we're grateful.

But still we are weary.

My heart, weighed down so long by my mother's suffering, soars with relief at her final rescue... joyfully leads the celebration of her life... revels in the assurance of God's eternal promise... and then crashes in sorrow and exhaustion, grieved by her absence and inundated by the sheer volume of "stuff" that needs attention.

There is no strength left to face what seems to be their cavalier indifference. Even so, it is clear God expects me to pursue peace.

I'd rather pursue new cultivars for my garden.

Nevertheless, my relentless Master commands me to obey Matthew 18 and go to those who wounded me; then warns that the only battle I may win is how I let Christ shine through me.

I need to die a whole lot more for that.

I am truly grateful—and relieved—when the two to whom I finally risk reaching out extend mercy and grace. But now I must <u>give</u> mercy and grace—their silence since those meetings feels like it was only to clear their own conscience. I believe their hearts are good and their concern was genuine. But the silence...

I need to die a whole lot more.

I'd rather plant flowers.

My garden is such a healing place when my Father meets me there and lets me lay my treasures at His feet. I know He wants obedience first. But when I ask Him to teach me courage and give me strength and help me learn to obey, He says, "I'll teach you brokenness and give you love and help you learn to die. Be still. Sit at My feet and let My Spirit heal you. Let me replace your hurt and anger with My love before you try to 'fix' anything—especially yourself."

The sad thing is, He wanted to bandage these wounds I've been complaining about a long time ago. They might have been healed by now if I had not kept pushing His hand away. I was so focused on who caused them and how much it hurt that I couldn't see the scars on hands that really wanted to help—the only ones that could. But now I see, and I am humbled and ashamed that—unlike His willful child—He never once said, "Look at the wounds <u>you</u> caused, you ungrateful little critter!"

Now my heart confesses it over and over: My wounds are nothing compared to the ones I caused Him, and I find in my Potter's wounded hand the answer to my deepest prayers: He is teaching me to obey Him better... trust Him more... and honor Him in all I do and say. He is teaching me to come and die... re-forming me to be a praise to His glory!

It is such an old, old story—such divine paradox! Only when I truly see Him can I dare to see me; an unworthy sinner made worthy only by His grace. Only when I finally give up my desperate search for some good in me and admit I deserve nothing but condemnation and death do I find the hope and liberty for which I've longed, and grasp the mystery that I really am infinitely valuable through His unfathomable love. Only when I finally give up my plans and desires and look to Jesus can I unconditionally embrace the death to which He calls me. And only when I finally give up my self and truly rejoice in the fellowship of His suffering can I experience His truth—death swallowed up by life!

His plans for me are good, to give me hope and a future. And most precious truth of all, His good plan is not just hope and a future, but His face reflected in me forever!

There are battles yet to come. Satan tells me I should be embarrassed and afraid to expose my weakness and selfishness. My pride will not go gently into that good night and *transparent and vulnerable* is dangerous; but I hope that seeing my worst "swallowed up by life" will be encouragement and rejoicing for those who love me (and maybe those who don't).

I'm still unclear how to pursue healing and restoration with those who may not want it. It is still hard to want to risk it. At this moment, I know those are just more opportunities for my Lord to be honored and glorified. He knows I want that with all my heart.

I'm not home yet, and I still have a whole lot more to die. But the ground at the foot of the cross is level and broad. Whether I go alone or meet others there, my Savior is waiting; ready to bless and forgive me. It's where I plan to be while He teaches me to live.

Chapter 2
of ADHDogs...

YESTERDAY, a funny thing happened at the foot of the cross. God reminded me I'm His ADHDaughter, and put the short leash back on. I thought—hoped—I was done with it, but the old me sneaked in and started running in circles again.

That "magic" leash is a fascinating phenomenon. At times <u>my</u> little ADHDog is uncontrollable, running in circles and bumping into walls, but the moment it is snapped to his collar he is a calm, sweet little fuzz ball, even when he is just dragging it around. Spanky wants to be outside where the big dogs are, but if we allow it, he will try to follow them down the road or run in circles until he is exhausted; so love demands the short leash.

Sometimes he resists. His little doggy brain knows we can use it to bring him up short and make him obey at any moment and he would rather be without it, but he knows it is his best chance to go outside, so he reluctantly surrenders.

I wish we could make him understand that obedience and submission bring safety and freedom. I wish we could look into those big brown eyes and explain there are dangers down that road where he so wants to run. I wish he would surrender and trust our authority so we could take that leash off. We would love to see him run free and play with abandon. But he just will not stay where he belongs, and we know what is down the road.

Will he ever be disciplined enough to stop running and obey our words? To choose his masters' will just to please us? To stay within our boundaries where he is safe? I hope he will. We won't quit working on him, because we chose him and he is ours, and we really love him.

I want to go outside where the big dogs are, but when my doggy nature impels me to run in circles or try to follow them down the road, Love demands the short leash again. Will I ever be disciplined enough to stop running and obey my Father's Word? To choose my Master's will just to please Him? To stay within His plan where I am safe? He promises me I will. I know He won't quit working on me, because He chose me and I am His, and He really loves me.

And He knows what is down the road.

... Parables & Puppy Dog Tales...

One can learn a lot from an ADHDog. This bright, sunny morning Spanky eagerly squeaks his favorite toy, demanding we play our usual game of fetch and tug; but I'm just not up to it. Old wounds re-opened and hope deferred have exhausted me, but I can't help smiling at his exuberance and energy. I'm weary with trying to believe something good really will come out of all this heartache, but this insufferably joyful creature will not be discouraged—it is time to play. And as we play, I hear my Father's voice: "Talk to Me, listen, watch... and learn..."

So I talk to Father God and try to listen, and He smiles His patience as He teaches ADHDog truths—again.

I tell Him I do not have strength or energy to face this—it just gets heavier all the time—and my Teacher whispers, "Learn from Spanky. His boundless energy isn't just 'Jack Russell.' You relish how he does everything with his whole being, and goes from full speed to sound asleep in an instant. But don't miss this important lesson: He rests as whole-heartedly as he plays, and always chooses to rest close to his master."

Keep Your ADHDaughter close, Master, until I learn to rest in You, wholeheartedly.

I know this is all a test, but I am so tired of fighting battles I can't win, and when I tell Him so, His answer humbles me. "Do you think Spanky loves to play tug-of-war because he believes he can win, or because he loves knowing you are on the other end?"

Help me remember You are on the other end of this, Immanuel!

My Father knows I truly want to obey Him—and for that to be enough. I understand obedience sometimes brings more hurt and humiliation. I heard His warning: "Hope for nothing more than a bridge as you risk reaching out." So we built a bridge, and those who wounded me are relieved. But all my old wounds came rushing back over that bridge and brought new ones with them, and I was not as prepared as I thought.

He hears my heart, and whispers another lesson: "Have you ever noticed how perfectly Spanky's favorite toy meets his needs? The designer knew exactly what it takes to keep a little dog challenged and growing. It is just strong enough to test his abilities, soft enough to comfort him, noisy enough to excite his energy, tough enough to withstand his pulling and tugging, light enough to carry wherever he is."

You'd give me nothing less, would You, Sovereign Designer!

To finally be free of that "short leash" I had to confront the truth, but this truth is so demeaning—and so bitter: Everything I did to honor God and every gifting He bestowed, they chose to treat as nothing more than trash to be thrown away. The truth is, that leash is a lot harder to tolerate when it is held by human hands.

The Truth is my Redeemer's plan. "Consider your little ADHDog. Study this gift one more time. You adopted him for your family's sake, but I gave him to you for your sake, to make you smile and help your heart heal. Now pay attention, and let him teach you My heart.

"See how enthusiastically he chases that toy, just because you throw it. Even if he ends up in a hard place, or crashes into a wall, he joyfully brings it back to you, eager to see where you will throw it next."

This hard place is just too uncomfortable, Abba, and I'm bruised from crashing into walls. Please restore to me the joy of Your salvation.

"Watch how eagerly Spanky listens for your voice, and how intently he searches your face when you simply speak his name."

Father, sometimes I can't hear You speak my name, no matter how I try. But I know nothing is more important, or privileged, than seeking Your face. Please give me ears...and eyes...

"Consider how gladly he chases <u>any</u> toy you throw, even though he treasures one special toy."

I want to believe new toys bring new joys, Lord. Help me remember it is all trash unless You choose it.

"Note when you play fetch how Spanky watches your hands so he will know which way to run."

It's hard to see Your hand in the dark, Master.

"Think how miserably he cries when you put him in his pen... how he hates the confinement and can't possibly understand your reasons. But you know it is where he is safe... that he will eventually wait peacefully on that pillow you provided, and greet your return with unreserved joy."

The "greeting Your return with unreserved joy" is easy, my Redeemer. It's the "waiting peacefully" where I need help.

"Watch how openly he communicates his needs... how completely he trusts you will care for him."

Thank You for wanting to hear my heart, Jesus, and for patiently, unrelentingly teaching me to trust You completely. I believe Your plan for me is good. Please, help thou my unbelief.

My Teacher helps my unbelief, and tells me this will be on The Final: "See how closely Spanky follows you, content just to be where you are? Consider how unconditionally he gives you his love, and freely claims yours. Think of your delight when he snuggles on your lap, totally secure in you. Do you think your relationship with your little dog is even a shadow of the relationship I plan with you?"

What can I say, Father! To be snuggled on Your lap is purest joy. I know You really love me. I'm so grateful You chose me and You won't quit working on me. I still yearn to go out and play with the big dogs, but You know what is down the road... and I still have a lot to learn from my little ADHDog.

... Playing with the Big Dogs...

I don't want to miss one thing my Father plans for me to learn, but I really yearn to play with the big dogs. I am so tired of standing here with my paws on the windowsill, wishing I was on the other side of this glass. I think an ADHDog can only be confined so long without losing heart. I want to <u>use</u> all this gifting and preparing and equipping He has been doing. I want to find out what is down that road, and I really think I'm ready to get out there where other dogs are running free.

But I hear my gracious Re-Former whisper, "Spanky." (I wonder if that's His new name for me.) I would rather obey than wear that leash again, so I'll try to wait peacefully on this pillow He provides. (At least there's more light here than in the pit.)

This time I hear Him speak my name. While I was whining to run free, He was freeing me to sing, and adding other voices to my song. He gives me ears, and tells me I just need to sing my song and re-learn a familiar verse: "*His thoughts are not my thoughts; His ways past finding out.*" He tells me it's OK I need to practice more—the score is much harder than before.

This time I see His hand. That glass I tried to look through was only "seeing darkly," and all I saw was me, looking back at me. He gives me eyes, and shows me that the road I want to follow would only take me farther from His plan. He knows what is down that road, and He is "making straight my path."

As usual, I would have settled for so much less. If I had been out playing with those dogs today, I would have missed rich prayer and priceless fellowship. If I had followed my own path, I would have squandered glorious time before His throne with old prayer-warrior friends, and never even have known I missed the privilege of new prayer partners He had waiting.

His plan for me is always good. His promise is secure. He tells me I could choose to run free now—He'd love me anyway and bless me where He could—but

I don't know what is down that road, and big dogs can be mean. He tells me that His pillow is filled with promise, and if I wait on Him, I'll soar on wings like eagles, run and not grow weary, walk and not be faint.

I think I'll wait.

...and Pity Parties when No One Comes

Who ever thought a pillow filled with promise could be so miserable! I really expected some relief when I finally resolved to "wait peacefully." But darkness returned in vengeance, with yesterday the darkest day of all.

I struggled to trust and say, like Job, "Though He slay me..." But I couldn't get past the "...I cannot be quiet! I am angry and bitter!" part.

I tried to remember that King David always ended his Psalm complaints with praise and thanksgiving, but my heart insisted, "...I believed, so I said, 'I am completely ruined!'"

I tried to cling to God's promise that *"...I will never leave you nor forsake you."* But, like Job, I looked everywhere and couldn't find Him.

I tried to accept that He is more concerned that I trust Him than that I feel Him. But Satan shouts in God's silence, and I can't withstand him alone.

I thought I should get up and do. Housework and garden chores are therapy. Other people need my touch. There are calls to make, and cards to send, and emails promised, but these months of struggle finally take their toll. My body is as sick as my soul, and it is all I can do to try to breathe.

I filled the day with prayer and scripture; studied books like Wilkinson's *Secrets of the Vine* and Warren's *Purpose Driven Life*, and articles like Olasky's "Life,

Liberty, and the Pursuit of Misery," and only felt more defeated than before.

I prayed harder, and walked the floor, and entreated God to give me just a touch. But bedtime came with tears that would not stop.

Then somehow during that long night, my heart found its voice: "Though he slay me, yet will I trust Him...I will praise the Lord Who counsels me... even at night my heart instructs me... His love endures forever... I will lie down and sleep in peace, for You alone, O Lord, make me dwell in safety..."

Today I see His hand.

Today I know He is most concerned that I trust Him, and understand that His silence is as loving as His touch.

Today I rest close to my Master and His pillow is soft and warm. (While my heart was praising Him in darkness, He was busy wrapping those scratchy promises in His peace.)

Today I trust that if I hope in Him, He will restore my strength. Today I know that if I wait upon Him, I will truly "see the goodness of the Lord in the land of the living."

Today I think I'll trust... and hope... and wait.

Chapter 3
on Healing Hearts...

IT SHOULD HAVE BEEN wonderful affirmation. Instead, it felt like the last painful straw. This woman whose life is such an example of God's mercy and grace... this self-described "hard nut" who has become a success by anyone's standards... this former pot smoker who now loves the Lord and gives Him all the credit... asserting how much she "owes me" for her growth and success. There was a time not so long ago I would have lived on that for days... weeks. I should have been honored to know God used me in her life. Instead, it felt like one more instance where He is blessing others while I have been used and thrown away. (I might as well admit it. He knows my every thought.)

I know it is a wake-up call. It is time to seek help.

My Father says, "In many counselors is wisdom." This counselor is especially wise—one to be heeded: "depression can become physical... physical illness needs treatment... you wouldn't try to just spiritually tough out a broken leg..." The analogy is valid. A broken heart is hazardous to the health, and often harder to mend, so why <u>do</u> we feel we have to "tough it out?"

I think it is this:

In our PCC (Politically Correct Christian) world a broken leg is PC. It is acceptable to acknowledge pain and even shed a few tears.

We can cry with the hurting,
> bring them food,
> pray with them,
> sympathize with how long healing takes,
> put a funny drawing on their cast,
> and go away glad we helped.

But a broken heart is <u>not</u> PC(C). We don't know what to do with that kind of pain.

> Crying over *feelings* is just embarrassing. (Christians are supposed to be strong and of good cheer, right?)
>> Casseroles seem incongruous,
>> prayer might bring more tears,
>> sympathy could make things worse, and
>> where do we put the funny drawing?
>> It is easier to stay away when we don't
>>> know how to help.

If confronting the heart pain of others is hard, exposing our own is terrifying. If it is our leg that is broken, we can "Christianly" acknowledge we need help and accept it as God's benevolence, but if it is our heart...well, we can't let others see that kind of weakness, can we?

The God of all comfort says Christ's sufferings overflow into our lives so we can "...comfort those in any trouble with the comfort we ourselves have received from God."

Another divine paradox, and a hard one to accept. Transparency is risky. Help may not come when we feel we need it most.

Nevertheless, the Father of compassion promises He will comfort me in all my troubles, and use them to bless others, so I determine not to let Him go until He blesses me. And He reminds me it wasn't a broken leg that caused Jacob's limp...

...Learning Lament...

God, where are you? God, if You love me, then why?

In his wonderful book, *A Sacred Sorrow,* Michael Card says those two questions lie at the heart of every lament—from Adam and Eve, to Job, to King David, to Jeremiah... to me. I have certainly asked them over and over. And God's answer seldom comes quickly—or easily.

I have always thought of the Friday Jesus was crucified as the darkest day for His disciples. But now I wonder if it was not actually the day <u>after</u> He died—that vacuum of time between the horrendous day we now call "good" and the glorious day of Life Resurrected. He had told them what to expect. They knew His promises. They had seen His power up close and personal. They had experienced His love "in spirit and in truth." But suddenly He was gone, and everything for which they had hoped and worked was gone with Him. It just did not make any sense... and these men and women who had sat at the very feet of the Master asked THE questions: *Jesus, where are You? Jesus, if You love us as You said, then why?*

Surely those dark hours were filled with lament—for all they had lost, and betrayals they could not deny. Their dark night of the soul was short. He came, and forgave, and answered their *why's.*

But I am learning that dark times of lament are a gift as wondrous as the light of His appearing... for them... and for me. Even though my dark night is still an Arctic experience. Even though every promise of dawn brings only cold half-light and then more darkness. Even though He comes, and forgives, and still hasn't answered my *why's.*

The Psalms have long been my refuge and teacher. I have prayed... grumbled... whined... sobbed... shouted... whispered those words of complaint and sorrow when I had no words of my own. I have been encouraged and humbled—and more than I want to admit, troubled—by the praise that ends those songs of lament.

But if every lament must end in praise... if, as Michael Card teaches, instead of lament being <u>a</u> path <u>to</u> praise and worship, it is actually <u>the</u> path <u>of</u> praise... if "the lost language of lament" is actually the bridge to His presence and sufficiency, then this journey begins to at last seem worth the price.

I think I still have much to learn before I am fluent in this "lost language." I think I still have much to die before I can welcome lament. I would much rather "be...of good cheer."

It is a bridge much too high for my comfort. I would really rather sit here, safely in the valley, and admire its lofty splendor. But I know the view from the top must be spectacular. So, I think I'll take the adventure I've been given and learn to speak this ancient tongue.

...and Walking the Talk

Truly it is an awe-filled thing to fall into the hand of the Living God! When I determined to learn this painful language and risk that "bridge too high," I didn't expect the very first step to be so threatening.

It is amazing how a tiny speck can hold such menace. This "just-something-to-watch" on Mac's lung has surprised his doctors—and us—and suddenly our lives are centered around it. They tell us it is probably benign, and they will only have to remove the nodule.

Encouraging words, until they tell us what the surgery itself entails. It could be, literally, a cure that kills! At best, it will be months before he is able to work again. But that little speck could be malignant, and the risk is too great to ignore.

So the date is set, and we are learning more than we want to know about lung cancer and life-saving surgery that can be lethal. But we are also learning... again...

... how to trust and pray in a deeper way than we ever have before;

... how crucial are the love and encouragement of family and friends;

... how very blessed we are that others pray for us; and

... how "peace that passes understanding" comes when Jesus prays for us.

Jesus prays for Mac! And me! And God is in control in this. His mercy exposed this threat at its earliest stage. His promises never fail. He will perfect that which concerns us. I know that we shall see the goodness of the Lord in the land of the living.

And that bridge looks higher with every step.

Chapter 4

of Hands that Build...

LAST NIGHT, when we were sharing that quiet, sweet dinner in that invitingly elegant Little Rock restaurant, my Father did it again!

Because we were trying so hard to ignore the elephant crowding everything else out of the room, I almost missed the gift He had tied to its tail. While we were struggling with the dread of this life-threatening surgery, God was using it to unwrap another delightful, profound truth.

It is so unmistakable and comforting as I face today, my heart bows before it... God treasures hands that build!

He has chosen and gifted hands to build from the beginning:

Noah's, for His ark of salvation...

Moses', for His tabernacle of consecration...

Solomon's, for His temple of worship...

Nehemiah's, to rebuild the wall for His city of hope.

He drew the blueprint and blessed their work, and then He used their hands to touch others.

And in this moment, waiting as other hands hold my husband's life and our future, praying God will guide their every touch, I think of how God has blessed his hands and his touch to bless others.

I think of all the businesses that operate a little more efficiently and staff who work a little more comfortably and safely because of his vision for how a structure should function—and his conviction it is always about the people in it.

I think of all the families whose lives are a little better because he invested heart and humor and wisdom, and never forgot he was building—or rebuilding—so much more than just a house.

I remember all the evenings of research and planning... all the phone calls and price comparisons and care for their investment... all the times he chose to go the extra mile... to give a little more and charge a little less... all the things that make all the difference... that didn't bother him a bit if no one knew but His Father (and me).

I think of the young men who enjoy bright futures today because he took the time to mentor and build up the gifts God designed in them.

I think of all the churches God has blessed and grown because he made sure the building they "lived in" was attractive and safe and strong—and more than worth the money they invested.

I think of my own life, and our kids', and know the homes we enjoy are blessed because of his giftings and generosity and heart for his family.

And I think that "carpenter" is a wonderful title to wear.

He's known that all along. He proudly states it: "I'm a carpenter." I confess I've thought he was selling himself short. I know how much knowledge and expertise and skill and creativity and responsibility go into every project he completes, and "building contractor" seemed to encompass all that so much better.

But now, in this bleak, plastic-upholstered place, tender Hands lay this latest gift in mine, and I am captivated by its elegance: It is no accident the Savior lived among us as a carpenter!

"In the beginning God created..." Then the Master Carpenter came to dwell among us, and spent most of His earthly life building... making lives better... touching and blessing people... doing all the things that make all the difference... that didn't bother Him a bit if no one knew but His Father.

He built up the gifts God designed in His people, built and blessed His Church, and then went back to build a house for His family to enjoy, forever.

It is no accident <u>my</u> carpenter's life reflects, in such a practical way, <u>the</u> Carpenter's...

...and I know "Carpenter" is a wonderful title to wear.

...and Reach for Help

God, I know You love me, but... why...?

I knew my minister friend was right. This is a hard thing to do alone, especially so far from home, and I was sure to "hit the wall" sooner or later. His daily calls have been "God with skin on," but yesterday's news was harder than I expected. Having to tell the kids their father has cancer was even harder. And having to face it alone was hardest of all.

Now this dilemma, at this time, in this crushing stillness, seemed especially cruel. It was not the first time my Father has allowed my computer to bring me to my knees. He knows I am only half joking when I declare "Satan lives in the computer." But its sudden crash when I needed it most was the agent of my sudden crash—and all I could do was kneel in that cheerless hotel room and cry, " *Why*, Lord?"

It was a good plan. I could mitigate our already-over-the-limit cell phone minutes (and my already-over-the-limit stress) if I updated everyone about Mac's progress by mass email instead of trying to return all those calls. (What blessing—all those calls! What testimony to God's love reaching out through His people. I was truly thankful, and told Him so over and over!)

So *why* would He not bless my desire to use our limited resources wisely?

Why would He not want all those people updated and praying specifically?

Why would He not protect me from this devastating delay when visitation in ICU is so limited? And most distressing of all,

why would He allow me to be so completely isolated, so far from home, at such a traumatic time, and then allow my most reassuring lifeline to be removed?

This time He answers my *why's* with His own, and demands an answer:

" *Why* do you think Mac is trying to "tough it out" instead of pushing the button that instantly delivers relief from his pain?"

Because he's vulnerable, and doesn't want to seem dependent or weak, Father?

" *Why* do his caregivers and you keep encouraging him to take advantage of whatever is available to 'stay ahead of the pain'?"

Because, Sovereign Lord, we really want the best possible outcome for him.

" *Why* do you sometimes reach over and push that button yourself, when he will not?"

Because, our Deliverer, I'm in a position to more clearly see what's best.

"And you are missing the lessons here for <u>you</u>... *Why*...?"

Could I "take the Fifth" on that, Teacher?!

It is time to face the truth—I am trying to "tough it out." It is not my computer that brought me to my knees—it is God's love, and when I finally decide to push my button for pain and confess I need help, He reaches over and pushes it for me. Relief is instant. Daughter Kellee calls—she's coming down. Both cell phones ring—people "just checking on us." My fickle computer comes musically to life and by His mysterious grace updates go out (along with my confession of need). But Sovereign God is not finished yet. He hits that button one more time and the "Red Sea" of interstate traffic parts. I am at the hospital just in time for Mac's joyful move out of ICU.

But here is another paradox: The very button everyone urged Mac to use for relief from pain has become the source of danger. His celebrated move out of ICU is cut short. The pump has malfunctioned. The pain reliever is making him "too comfortable" and he is not breathing deeply enough to ward off pneumonia. So, it is alarmingly, disappointingly back to ICU to remove his reassuring lifeline, before it kills him.

I'm not going to miss the lesson this time, my Provider. You are the God of Mercy, and only You know which mercies I need each morning.

The paradox applies: The very button He gave me to use for relief from pain could become the source of danger if it makes me "too comfortable" and I'm not breathing His Holiness deeply enough to ward off fallenness. My disappointing move back to "intensive care" was to remove my reassuring lifeline, before it killed me. And He reminds me again that nothing is ever wasted in His economy—especially pain.

Chapter 5
ADHDogs & Scooter

WE LAUGHED that our daughter was at it again, but I'm so glad she didn't give up. She insisted this was what Spanky needed to settle him down—dogs are pack animals—they need other dogs. He really was one of the cutest little puppies I had ever seen, but if one ADHDog dominated our home, what would happen with two? Her father just did not think we needed another one. (I reminded him that is what he had said about the first, and the truth came out: What if Spanky felt "left out"—pushed aside by this intruder in his kingdom? What if we couldn't really love two dogs?) But this father could never resist his youngest's big blue eyes, and before we knew it, we were headed home with another furry little critter—vowing to "only try it a day or two."

Within "a day or two," our little ADHDog and this Definitely-Not-ADHDog were inseparable, endlessly running and romping and tugging on the same toy. And within a day or two, we were in love with this Always Happy Dog—so like his half-brother and yet so different.

Spanky is a running, jumping, let-me-at-'em object lesson that always makes me smile, even when his ADHDog nature wears me out.

Scooter is a snuggling, tail wagging, let-me-kiss-you study in opposites that always makes me laugh out loud, even if it is just to see his shaggy little face. He is such a happy, loving, uncomplicated little creature. Life is so much easier for him—and us. No short leash needed in his world. He runs free and unconstrained. His master's voice is all it takes to keep him in our boundaries where he's safe.

While Spanky's stubborn will still drives him to that dark glass, Scooter's gentle nature draws him to our feet.

While Spanky still whines for whatever is outside, Scooter nestles on my lap, content to just be close.

While Spanky seeks our love because we make him obey, Scooter obeys because he wants our love.

Their antics bring us joy, and we could not love them more. But our Father always has a bigger plan. These bright-eyed mischief makers are angels of mercy from His hand—instruments of healing for this long, slow convalescence. How they bring about healing, who can say; but Mac's lifted spirits and lowered heart rates testify that they do, and my heart smiles to see two little white balls of energy quietly snuggling with him as he rests. I watch two usually-unguided missiles settle oh-so-carefully on either side of him in his recliner, and think God surely must be whispering, "Gently, now!"

Unexpected gifts are my Father's love in action. We could have so easily refused these sweet companions and never have known the healing joy He had for us. Mac might have missed the cheer and restoration they bring him every day. I might have had to learn so many things in much less gentle ways. My Teacher tells me there are lessons yet to come: "Watch a little closer. Spanky's little brother is not so simple as he seems..."

I love these little lessons wrapped in fur. I know they're gifts from God. But when my Teacher asks if I've considered how unreservedly Spanky welcomed this sudden change in his safe little world, I wish we could start with a less convicting question.

Still, one can learn a lot from an ADHDog, and Scooter.

Chapter 6
Sweet Memories & Hard Truths...

IT JUST SEEMED GOOD to go back one more time. That charming, elegant restaurant holds sweet memories.

It is where we took refuge and "strengthened wobbling knees" to face the unthinkable. It is where God began unwrapping a deeper appreciation for my husband's calling... where my daughter and I found peace in the storm and chased away the elephant—for a while. It seemed important to have dinner there while we were back in Little Rock for Mac's all-important follow-up.

The hotel was another matter.

It was the logical place to stay: great location, easy access to the VA Medical Center, hospital discount. But it is where I wrestled demons I do not want to remember. The bleakness of those rooms infected (reflected?) my spirit, and I dread another day alone in that environment, waiting for the doctors to "do their thing," praying for a good outcome. But I will never really be able to make Mac understand how much I am affected by my surroundings, so practicality trumps emotions, and I remind myself that nothing is wasted in God's economy...

...even ugly hotel rooms in pretty settings.

If this "pretty on the outside, ugly on the inside" paradox troubles me so much, there is a warning here. If I fear demons I have already seen God defeat, those hard-fought battles may be far from over. If bleak surroundings really can make my spirit bleak, or an evening in gracious surroundings heal it, I may be headed for another ICU experience.

The irony is, both hold the same lesson: Sweet memories and hard truths and deep revelations all reside in the heart. God chooses pleasant and unpleasant places alike for His purpose—to bless us with tears and teach us to praise and draw us closer to Him.

And just outside both doors I find the path to the bridge...

...and Rainbows & New Mercies

According to the wise man, there is nothing new under the sun. I am so glad he wrote that so many centuries ago, since there is nothing new in this observation—just an overflow of my heart that must be expressed.

The post-op result is better than we dared hope. The cancer is gone! No chemo or radiation therapy is needed! We are both truly grateful, but exhaustion and the long recovery ahead obscure everything else.

The lake house deck is my sanctuary. I wait for the healing tranquility of the dawn, and God blesses me with my favorite of mornings. Mist shrouds the tree-covered hills. The lake is like polished glass. The rising sun shines on dark, towering thunderheads, turning sky and water to intense, luminous blue. The stillness is so soft and deep it swallows every sound but the thunder rumbling in the distance.

I wrap my praise in His Word and celebrate that "...the heavens declare the glory of God!"

He wraps this morning in blessing, and "...the earth shouts forth His handiwork!"

At first I thought the rosy column on the hills across the lake was the reflection of cell tower lights on the clouds. That would have been enough. The effect was stunning. But in the next instant, His glory declared itself in a spectacular rainbow; vibrant and iridescent and achingly fleeting. I covet its radiance for my clouded spirit and wish it would last; but as usual, His ways are not my ways. My towering thunderheads dissolve to featureless gray, my rainbow fades, and class is in session.

It is a short lesson—nothing new under the sun except His morning mercies and old truths re-stated.

Unanticipated rainbows are the Father's love revealed. They often come when we need them most and deserve them least, but we do not get to choose the time or design. If we want the rainbow, the clouds must come. Dark, dramatic, "Psalm 29" ones are exciting—definitely my favorite—but gray, humdrum ones bring the most life-giving rain. Though we see only the undersides of them, especially on endless, gray, no-rain days, we are always just one sunbeam away from a rainbow, no matter how dark or gray the clouds. His promise is eternal, and His light always shines through at just the right moment for the truest colors; but unless we are looking up, enjoying the clouds, we will miss the rainbow.

The wise man says there is nothing new under the sun, but I know the Painter of the rainbow, and His mercies are new every morning.

Chapter 7
Manna Every Morning...

THE PROBLEM WITH MANNA is that you have to go out and pick it up every day. Sometimes I would like to save up just a little, for the times I am too tired, or too discouraged, (or maybe too lazy) to go find it. But (here is the paradox) the blessing of manna is that it is so *daily*. If I could save it up, all too soon I would forget how much I need the Giver of my daily bread. If I didn't have to go out to get it, I would miss a lot of little desert flowers along the way. And if I wrote the menu, I would never know the exciting cuisine God has waiting.

I am thankful for another grant review assignment. It is some of the hardest work I've ever done, and not how I would like to spend the entirety of my working life, but I always come away grateful for the manna God has tucked away in the most unexpected places.

This Sunday afternoon trip to Washington, DC, is even more exhausting than usual. Monday morning orientation and all-day training are mandatory, and it is doubtful I will be allowed to do this review if I miss the day. But my flight is three hours late and my Chicago connection is long gone. The only available flight—on any airline—will not arrive in DC until Monday evening. Exhaustion and frustration overwhelm me after an agent gives the wrong gate for standby. A needless trip around the concourse adds insult to injured, aching feet, and results in my being last on a very long list; but my Advocate is at work! Somehow my name is called, and the fragrance of manna is sweet as I settle into the very last available seat on the very last flight out.

...Sometimes at Midnight...

The trip to the Washington National Conference Center is... interesting. I am always impressed with the organized chaos of Dulles International. I'm relieved when my bag appears on the conveyer—miraculously on the plane at the last minute, too—and glad they still have someone to shuffle this long line of weary travelers into cabs in the middle of the night.

Though a cab driver I can't understand is nothing new in this hub of international activity, a speeding cab that keeps drifting off this deserted road while he re-programs his GPS is 'way more excitement than I want at this late hour. I am so relieved to finally see the Center's security gate, but this manna experience is just beginning. (It must be the hand of God. Manna spoils after midnight, doesn't it?)

There is no "McReynolds" on the security guard's list, and as I contemplate how I am going to find a place to stay until morning, my cab driver redeems himself. He shows her my "official" itinerary—the one I handed him so he could find this place in the middle of nowhere. She accepts it "for now," and hands it back with just enough manna to get me through the next step on this middle-of-the-night adventure.

There is no "McReynolds" on the reservation list at the lodge, either; but the magic itinerary does its job again, (I'm beginning to think it is made of manna paper) and the friendly clerk eventually finds me a room and hands me a map: We are in the "North Building" but my room is in the "South"—a real problem, since there are also "East" and "West" and unmarked buildings on that map, and even "left and right" are sometimes tricky for this directionally-challenged woman. But God keeps the manna coming, even in the dark, and in spite of this confusing labyrinth of buildings, feet that protest every step, locked doors, security guards who never come, and an even more confusing labyrinth of inside corridors, at three a.m. I finally stumble into the right room in the right building, and not long after, find myself asking God for a little manna for the man who knocks on my door, also just assigned to this room.

...in Desolate Places...

The appointment is wrong. We all know it, and hope the hesitant, soft-spoken woman will step down. We have experienced the problems an ineffective panel chair can bring in this time- and work-intensive, meticulously detailed environment before. It is puzzling they would select someone so obviously ill-equipped and overwhelmed with the responsibility. Equally puzzling that she chooses to accept.

By Wednesday the panel is floundering. Not one review is completed. But we cry with her when she is called out and comes back to report—in tears—that she will be stepping down. The humiliation seems so needless, the extra work of catching up so senseless.

But God has the manna basket out, and over the next few days we are blessed by this quiet woman's dignity and grace as she chooses to stay on as a panel member; and we feast on wonderful fellowship and teamwork, get the work out on time, and draw together in a way we never would have but for this.

...and Crowded Skies...

It is a troubling thing, but I find myself understanding the Children of Israel 'way too much! I really am thankful for God's wonderful provision throughout this project, but right now I just do not want any more manna.

I am too exhausted to want anything more than to fall into my assigned seat, slide my new hi-tech computer case under the seat in front of me, and sleep. (Never mind that hi-tech case is too wide to roll down the narrow aisles of this jumbo jet, or that my seat is almost all the way in the back, on the opposite side. At least it is on an outside row, on the aisle.)

I just do not have the heart to tell the woman already sitting there (in <u>my</u> seat!) I won't trade so she can sit by her friend, so I console myself hers is at least on an aisle, too... until I realize that the center aisle, eight-across seats with no arms are too small to slide anything under, and neither sleep nor work are an option surrounded by fifty(!) wiggling, giggling, chattering, paper-wad-throwing kids. My generosity begins to fray when I discover that the woman had been assigned to this seat as their chaperone, and almost unravels as she continues to chat with her friend, oblivious to the two girls who excuse themselves past me for their third trip to the bathroom, followed by the three boys next to them who could have much more easily exited on their end of the aisle.

God never over-rides our free will, but I've discovered He sometimes—in His mercy—unmercifully prods! He has "unmercifully" rewarded my "generosity" with a hard place, where I can do none of the things I wish. But for once I really mean it when I say, "OK, Lord...Your will," so Mercy blesses me indeed, and enlarges my territory. All three young men apologize profusely for bothering me as they return to their seats, and the rest of the flight, smile whenever I glance their way. The sweet-faced girl next to me leans over and whispers, "I'm sorry if we bothered you. She doesn't feel good, and I didn't want to let her go alone."

Exhaustion fades with the pleasure of (finally) watching teens in every seat around me just being kids. Good-natured teasing embellishes chatter about their trip. Paper wads aim at each other only, and when one happens to bounce into my lap, a simple look from that apparently inattentive chaperone brings a quick "Sorry!" from both kids. Then suddenly I am surrounded by fifty carefree young faces animated by a hundred perfectly choreographed hands and shoulders, silently, joyfully "dancing" to the music in their headphones. And as the flight ends, fifty tee-shirted boys and girls patiently wait to collect bags and backpacks until all the other passengers de-plane, as do fifty more in the next section.

I can't leave without complimenting them—and their sponsors—for their courtesy and good example, but as I smile my way down the jet way, hi-tech computer bag rolling obediently behind, Mercy brings my heart to its knees.

"Has it occurred to you that I have just given you a privileged seat in the middle of your mission field? For whom have you poured out your life the last twenty years? What have you just spent the last two weeks—and others this year—doing? Do you think one of the abstinence education grants you've recommended might possibly help reach some of <u>these</u> kids with life-changing truths they would never find any other way?"

So, humbled, my grateful heart lays this confession before Him: Nothing is ever wasted in His economy, even tired bodies and tiny aisle seats and wiggling, giggling, dancing teens in crowded jumbo jets.

...with Water from the Rock

I have to admit, by now I dread the question. It is not the answer I want to give: "Not a clue where God is taking me... no real prospects for the future!"

This friend has been encourager, counselor, and confronter through this long, dark night, and wants almost as much as I do to see that bigger, better thing all my friends insist God has for my life. It would be so much less humiliating if I could point to it and say, "I knew all along He was getting me ready..." So much less painful if I had that "bigger and better" to turn to. So much easier to reject Satan's whispers that God is through with me... is not going to use me anymore... probably never did as much as I want to believe...

Besides, I don't want to disappoint. So many friends have invested so much love and concern and prayer. I want their investment to bring a huge return. I want them to be encouraged and excited about what they see in this pain. I want an inspiring testimony of God's bounty, "...pressed down, running over." Like the woman I met on the DC shuttle last week.

She certainly overflowed with excitement over God's bounty in her life—this 21st Century, degreed and credentialed African-American woman, larger than life in every way, impeccably groomed, expensively dressed and jeweled, dynamic and friendly and exuding confidence.

She knew with certainty it was God's intervention that made her miss the previous, crowded shuttle and put us together on this one with no one else aboard.

She bubbled over with enthusiasm for the new, world-wide ministry to women God was using her to establish. She had no doubt I would figure in that somehow, even though we had only met five minutes ago.

She gave God all the glory for moving her to just the right facility... in just the right city... and giving her just the right house... already decorated in her colors... on a golf course... with a beautiful garden and a huge fountain and a private waterfall cascading down her private hillside... and the Prayer of Jabez in the powder room! As we said good-bye she took my email address and promised to write.

I doubt that she will.

But my heart is with another African-American woman beside whom I have just spent the week working. She is also certain God brought our lives together. She is also in ministry. She is also confident of God's reality and presence in her life.

But there the similarities end. Her life bubbles over with pain and disappointment. She struggles with rejection and an uncertain future. The husband she's trusted God would restore to her has just married another woman, though he is still married to her. The source of income she has counted on through these grant reviews has just evaporated, in spite of her hard work and excellent leadership, for no apparent reason.

It took almost all week, but at the end He brought us together to pray, and we loved each other as sisters— and rejoiced that our lives were connected for eternity. I took her email address and promised I would send her my "journal." As we waved good-bye, she shouted "...love you!" one last time and we pledged to pray for each other and stay in touch.

I know that we will.

My Father loves to give good gifts to His children. I'm thankful for new friends in unexpected places, and I contemplate how one draws me to <u>herself</u> and lets me see her victory while the other draws me to her <u>Jesus</u> and lets me hold her hand. I am humbled by this wounded warrior's transparency and courage, and appreciate a little better how blessed we are in this "fellowship of suffering."

And I recognize... again... that this stiff-necked child is in the desert for a reason. It is too easy to shake my head at the foolish Children of Israel—fed every day by the very Hand of God, feasting on the bread of heaven and grumbling for something different—and still fail to see that same hand, scarred by my sin, full of my daily bread.

I am ashamed that the foolishness of Israel is mine. I hunger for the things of Egypt—those "bigger, better things" to validate and vindicate and prove my worth. He wants to feed me, day by day, bread of heaven still warm from His touch. He has struck the Rock to give me living water so I will never thirst again. But still I stumble in the desert—still can't quite comprehend why the Creator of Heaven and Earth waits for <u>me</u>... every morning... with "good gifts!" And I hear Him whisper, "Don't wait until you understand. Just come."

So, I think I'll find out when the manna bus leaves. On second thought, I think I'll walk. I want to look up and enjoy those clouds. Maybe I'll see a rainbow. Maybe those little desert flowers are still blooming. Maybe the trail leads back to my bridge

Chapter 8
the Problem of Scooter

HE IS STILL ONE of the cutest little dogs I have ever seen—this fuzzy little "fat boy"—as dear to us now as his brother. But our tail-wagging purveyor of doggy kisses hides a surprisingly dark secret. This gentle, teachable, obedient little guy—so different from his frenetic, willful, challenging sibling—is riddled with envy! Whether it is Spanky, Mac, my computer, or something else demanding my attention, he is impelled to insert himself between us. He has never really cared for the toys Spanky still scatters around the house like a two-year-old, unless it is the one with which Spanky wants to play. We cannot help but laugh at him—it is so blatantly, childishly "me first."

But Father whispers, "Careful... heed this warning: What is so cute and laughable in Scooter is dishonoring and deadly in My children."

I want to hang my head in shame and dive behind the pillow where Scooter hides, hoping with him that no one will see we are in trouble ...again!

It is easy to shake one's head at people like the "Virginia Tech shooter," so overcome by envy and resentment he was driven to kill again and again. But what about my competitive spirit, my compulsion to achieve, my perfectionist tendencies, my longing to be included in the exciting ministries that seem closed to me? Aren't they just branches of the same bitter root? I hear Him warn that they are—and the soil that nurtures such a bitter root is hard and dangerous ground.

My Teacher told me there were doggy lessons yet to come. But who would have thought my Always-Happy Dog would bring such not-so-happy truths: This heart that wants so much to honor God still strives for vindication—and shrinks at His reproof. There's not much room behind this pillow where Scooter goes to hide, but I dread to face my Father with this sin... again.

And then I hear His tender voice, "Let's review these ADHDog-and-Scooter truths again. (I remind you, it is on the test.) Remember how I use your little dogs to illustrate My Grace. Consider your relationship with them—you know it models Mine with you. Are you forgetting how much you enjoy just loving them, or how it pleases you when they seek your favor, or how gladly you forgive and bless them? Why do you keep expecting less from Me!? Talk to Me, listen... and repent."

And as I try to find my voice to tell Him that I'm sorry, He smiles through trusting big brown eyes and little doggy kisses, and I can't help but laugh out loud.

My little AHDog and I still have a lot to learn—this pillow still might tempt. I think we'll trade it for that other one... the one our Master filled with scratchy promises; then wrapped up in His peace.

Chapter 9
More Paths to the Bridge...

NOTHING IS WASTED in God's economy—even sleepless nights, and paths that appear to lead nowhere. If pain is the path of praise, sleeplessness is a stepping stone along the way... or at least it seems it should be. The night-time quiet of this home should be a wonderful, welcoming environment to seek God's face. The warmth and comfort of this bed should be reason enough to offer Him thanks. I remember telling my kids to "think pretty thoughts" when they couldn't sleep; but the fact is, random thoughts and runaway emotions attack best in the dark, with inexplicable dread that knots the gut.

I struggle to "take every thought captive," but restless muscles and aching head distract and fragment those thoughts.

I vow to follow King David's example and praise God "on my bed," but after only a few "thankfuls" old hurts and fears I thought were resolved are back with a vengeance, and the darkness is anything but quiet and comforting.

Spoken thoughts are easier to take captive, so I slip out of my warm bed and head downstairs to my "prayer chair." My Father waits for me there, and my heart knows what a precious gift His presence is. But the darkness waits for me there, too, and in spite of my best efforts, this night-after-night struggle becomes one of dread and anxiety and defeat. The accuser's voice just will not be stilled, even in my Protector's presence.

Then once again I see God's blessed, painful paradox. He leads me on this dark path. It is where I must confront my fearful, ungrateful heart. It is where I will come, at last, to His bright bridge of repentance and forgiveness. This paradox is Joseph's prison...Isaiah's vine... Jeremiah's cistern... David's cave. It is agreeing in faith to grieve the loss of my heart's desire as long as my Father deems necessary—to embrace it as part of His plan and count it all joy—without resentment or rebellion. It is living day by day, re-learning trust moment by moment. And it is recognizing and celebrating that having to come back to Him for each day's serving of faith is a wondrous gift to bring me into the Very Presence for which I long.

Lord, I believe. Thank You for helping my unbelief.

...with Blisters along the Way

"I think maybe you've lost some of your gratitude for all God has done in your life."

Hard words to hear, but this counselor's wisdom has served God's purpose in my life for years, and I know he is right. I really didn't want that kind of counsel right now. I want reassurance that this latest "loss" is not just more of the pattern in my life that haunts me. This work embodies the passion and calling I still know with all my heart is God given. It was not I who raised my expectations to be a part of it—and now it is a shattering rebuff to be so cavalierly "included out" without explanation or compassion. This church that has been home, refuge, teacher, encourager, is now the source of new wounds over old.

But when I reach out for restoration and healing, the rebuke is harsh: "This isn't about you!" Most certainly true. It is about Kingdom work—so much bigger than I can conceive. Indisputably, serving God in any way is always privilege—never a right. But isn't Kingdom work also about "bear[ing] one another's burdens... weep[ing] with those who weep... encourag[ing] one another daily..." and healing the "aught[s] against any[s]?" Can God be glorified when His church shoots its wounded? Are we only worthy of concern when we are "useful?" And who defines "useful?" What qualifies (or disqualifies) one for consolation and care in His body? My if-then, cause-and-effect nature demands answers, even as self-doubt shrinks from what I might not want to hear. But I know this truth is fundamental: As long as I let it be "about me," I will miss what God has planned.

So, Jesus, please pray for me. I know You love me just as I am—weak and needy and flawed. You will perfect that which concerns me, and I'm grateful You will do whatever it takes to bring me back to Your cross. You tell me that You want only all I have left—a broken will and teachable spirit and open, contrite heart.

Lord, I believe... and I am gaining new appreciation for the prayer embodied in that scripture. "Help Thou my unbelief..." is a deeper, wider, riskier petition than I can comprehend.

I choose You, my Unsafe, Jealous, Wildly Loving Savior. Help Thou my unbelief. And please, my Kind Redeemer, this one thing more... give me a grateful heart.

Chapter 10
of Purpose-Driven Pain

ANY CHRISTIAN who has been through even one crisis of pain has heard it ad nauseum: "Lean into the pain... let God teach you all He wishes through it." Of course it is true. It is what this journey journal is all about, but it is only human to want it to be <u>over</u>. Pain is so... painful!

Former Indianapolis Colts coach Tony Dungy said of his then-five-year-old son, whose life is always in danger because he has no pain receptors, "We've learned that a lot of times because of that pain, that little temporary pain, you learn what's harmful. You learn to fear the right things."

And God reminds me that even my "long, dark night" is just "little temporary pain" in light of eternity. If He protected me from it (I confess I still too often wish He would), I would never learn to fear the right things.

So, I guess I'd better work on "learning what's harmful."

Maybe a few more blisters will finally teach me not to touch those coals of rebellion again.

Surely stumbling over a few more rocks will finally teach me to walk carefully along this path of praise.

Maybe I can finally thank Him for these blisters.

Maybe I can even begin to "lean into the pain."

Chapter 11
His Presence in the Wilderness...

SINCE THE BEGINNING of this journey, I've encouraged and consoled myself in the lives of Moses... Caleb... Joshua... especially King David. Though my desert experience is but an instant compared to forty years of living there and forty more of wandering (I hope) and I will never come even close to doing "mighty deeds;" there is reassurance in seeing how God uses worn and wearied people for His purpose.

I can't really relate to Moses—that "greatest prophet" God knew face-to-face. But I've often wondered... before I AM brought him barefoot and tongue tied to that holy bush, did Moses ever question why He rescued and equipped him for royal leadership, only to abruptly isolate and "dead end" him in the desert? By the end of forty desert years, had he just resigned himself to living out his days there as a simple shepherd? Did he ever wish for the excitement and privilege of his former life?

And then after Yahweh had used him in such powerful ways... when he had conquered Pharaoh's mighty armies with just his staff and trust in God... when he had led his Father's rebellious children out of idolatry and through that fearsome desert... wouldn't he have expected to hear "well done?"

So, when God told him he would never enter the Promised Land and refused his final plea to "let [him] go over," did he ever think it was too harsh a price for just one mistake in a life God Himself called "like no other?" As he climbed that final desolate mountain alone, did he feel disappointed or cheated or sad?

This thought troubles and confuses me: Though he sinned (we all have), Moses served God with all his heart and might and wanted only to finish His work and glorify Him in His holy land. So why would God condemn him to die alone, denied the greatest longing of his heart?

I can relate to David. His struggles are mine. His sins I've committed. His Psalms speak my heart. If God could find in him "a man after [His] own heart," there is still hope for me! But I've struggled with that same sad (resentful?) confusion about his life. His greatest desire was to glorify God—his psalms still sing His praise today. His greatest dream was to build His house of worship. So why would God deny his dream and give it to another?

There is no paradox in His answer. It is clear and unconditional. He is God, and Sovereign God will choose.

Gracious Mysterion did choose: "Deny" their human hearts' desire, and give them His divine.

Immanuel chose to fill up Moses' longing with Himself! Can you picture them, walking arm in arm along that lonely mountain path? Standing on the mountain top, admiring that long-sought land through God's own holy eyes? Can you see Tender Grace and Love carry Moses home and then bury his used-up body with His own holy hands?

God-With-Us chose to fill up David's yearning heart as well. Can you see Him at the table, helping David draw the plans for his great shining vision? Can you hear Him tell this man of His own heart that though David will not get to build the House of God, God Himself will build the House of David, to bring the world salvation through His Son!

Here is the marvelous paradox: In the end, both God's greatest prophet and Israel's mightiest king stood stripped of every worldly power and privilege. But when God's "no" led to the wilderness, they chose to honor Him with humble, trusting praise. Both wrote their greatest psalm out of that barren place. And after they had nothing left to give, He filled them up with Heaven's Greatest Gift.

So must I choose. As Moses and David ultimately did, I'll bow my knee in trust and joy, or be brought down in sorrow.

And on my knees I find my Jesus kneeling there! He prays for me, and shows me this amazing truth: Life's deepest yearnings and hope's most cherished dreams are small exchange indeed, when Holy Presence comes to fill a broken heart.

...with Praise in the Tempest

I do love a good thunderstorm. My heart can't help but shout His praise as the thunder comes rumbling closer and closer and lightning flashes all around. It is such a magnificent display of his power and might. But to be honest, I don't want to be outside during one, especially on a boat in the middle of Table Rock Lake on the Fourth of July.

If you have never been there, nothing is more breathtaking than fireworks over the water! Spectacular bursts of brilliance jewel the sky and illuminate the elegant arches of Central Crossing Bridge. Red and green and white running lights from countless boats reflect in the water as far as one can see. Cheers and horns applaud stunning pyrotechnic wonders. Barges draped with red-white-and-blue bunting slowly cruise through the throng, playing patriotic music and showcasing living "statues of liberty." Chamber of Commerce members follow behind, selling patriotic tee shirts to pay for next year's display.

I love it all—the pageantry, the celebration of liberty, the fellowship of freedom—even all the hype. But for years it has been tainted by my dread of the return trip. No matter how I've tried to conquer it (nonstop verses of scripture and "Master the Tempest is Raging" are no help at all) my lifelong fear of the water becomes sheer terror in the midst of churning waves from all those boats, rolling unexpectedly out of the dark and tossing our usually-stable pontoon rig about like a toy.

But Mac had promised this year we would wait as long as we needed to be sure all the traffic was gone, and I was determined to finally trust God with this fear I've always known is totally irrational. For the first time in years, I was truly looking forward to every part of the evening, even when those "just little clouds going the other direction" became big clouds headed right for us. And as we watched lightning play over the mountain, I was even able to laugh about God's fireworks—so much better than the ones a storm might cut short. But hope still springs eternal, and like most of the other boaters, we waited, hoping it would move on past before dark.

Then, a torrent of rain roared down the lake, sweeping away all hopes of celebration, and we joined the swarm of vessels racing for home. In moments it was evident there would be no navigating in this blinding downpour, so we headed for the floating restaurant we knew was mercifully just around the bend.

Three generations of our kids have loved eating on The Port Restaurant's canopied deck, throwing dinner morsels over the rail to watch the scrappy ducks outmaneuver their regal cousins while giant carp, elegant perch, tiny minnows, and surprisingly quick turtles cruise around them, waiting for their chance to snatch a french fry or tidbit of lettuce. As we pulled into the slip and scrambled for that familiar deck, now dark and deserted, it had never seemed more inviting. But though shelter from the pounding rain was a blessing, I found myself gratefully surprised that our mad dash through the storm had seemed like... <u>fun</u>!

Now I sat on the soggy, forlorn dock on an ugly plastic chair (they'd always seemed quite festive in the light), soaked from head to toe and freezing (on the Fourth of July!), gratefully sipping the hot coffee Mac never leaves home without, and longing for my warm, dry bed. Sooner or later this deluge had to move on, but for now it still swept across the lake in great, blinding sheets. Then suddenly those magnificent curtains of rain shouted His Glory into my heart, and swept His Spirit over me with "joy unspeakable!"

My heart no longer whimpered at the raging tempest and roiling waters. Instead it shouted, "The Voice of the Lord is enthroned over the flood! ...Blessed be the name of the Lord!"

He is that "Perfect Love [that] casts out fear." Truly. And at least this time, I chose Perfect Love...and cast out fear. What victory! What pleasure! (What relief!) But what sorrow to know I've refused so many other chances to glorify Him in my weakness.

So-o-o... Is my fear of water a thing of the past? Will I be able to get out of the boat and walk on the water when He calls? Or will I still panic in the storm and accuse Him of not caring if I perish? Only my Father knows for sure, but He promises He'll be with me always, and tonight I praise Him that my puny tempests are no match for the Master of the storm.

Chapter 12
the Bridge~from a Ruined Life

IT JUST CAME OUT OF NOWHERE—this renewed grief that is totally unexpected and terribly disappointing. It has been such a good week, and for once I've been steadfast to tell my Father how very grateful I am for His mercy and grace. And always He is faithful, an ever present help, in the storm or in the wilderness.

But here is His glorious, mysterious paradox (again): His greatest provision will sometimes be His absence. His sweetest gift may be this lament that forces me to finally, as Michael Card says, let go of "the ruins of a once whole life" so I can at last offer Him purest praise that comes out of a heart emptied of everything but Him. Is it possible I could ever praise Him with such delicious praise? Can my heart extend a worship that welcomes the wilderness... where Jesus hears... and comes... and shares our suffering? Can I truly, honestly <u>choose</u> this grief as His sweet gift? Can I finally relinquish all I am so He can, at last, fulfill my heart's desire and make me a praise to His glory?

Maybe only tear-filled eyes can see that shining bridge on which I long to stand.

So from my forlorn cave that overlooks my ruined life, I choose your glorious, terrible path, Lord. I cannot wait to see the view from the bridge.

Chapter 13
Principalities & Powers

" *I HAVE COME because of your words.*"
Strange how one can miss the most significant of statements in scripture until God puts it where you finally stumble over it. I've known the story of the angel God sent to Daniel—delayed three weeks by the "prince of the kingdom of Persia"—since my VBS days. I've envisioned the cosmic battle that must have occurred when the prince of the Kingdom of Heaven came to help and they finally broke through. Of course I've understood that God honored Daniel's fast and heard his prayer. And I've been surprised and perplexed that Satan's minions could have such power that they could delay God's messengers. It is a reality I disregard at my peril. If God's mighty warriors had to struggle against principalities and powers, who am I to think I could, for one moment, survive outside the protection of my Father's wing!

But I don't remember ever really <u>hearing</u> this passage before. The angel told Daniel that from the first day he set his heart to understand (I like that part—my Teacher knows how my heart is set on understanding) and humbled himself before God, (He knows my heart is set on that, too, even if He still too often has to do the humbling) *his words were heard.* Why does this seem so new, when I know God hears our every thought? And

56

why does the angel's coming because of Daniel's words seem so significant?

Here is the awesome, illuminating truth: God hears our every thought. He sees our every need. He knows our very heart. But our <u>words</u> move His hand.

I've known for many years one of my assignments from Him is prayer "warrior-ship." I cherish that assignment. I really do appreciate what a privilege it is to come before the throne of the King—and know He welcomes me there. But too often I fail to faithfully carry out that assignment. Is opposition from principalities and powers the reason—or my own weak, lazy, rebellious, negligent heart? I think the answer is yes.

I must speak my petitions before Him. Whether He comes in three seconds, weeks, years—or even decades—is His sovereign business. Mine is to faithfully persevere, and believe He will come.

But here is the mysterious, demanding paradox: I can neither come before Him faithfully, speak my prayers honestly, nor trust He will come, without His empowering presence. To paraphrase the great apostle, "Oh wretched [wo]man that I am! Who will rescue me..."

Of course, He already has. And He patiently, persistently teaches me this same fundamental assurance: I choose, and He works in me to will and to do according to His good pleasure. And if the best I can do at any given time is just speak the "want" to choose, He will come, and complete what He began in me.

So this gorgeous, rainy Autumn day, I choose to speak. Please, King of Heaven, breathe life and faithfulness into my speaking, and come because of my words.

Chapter 14
of God-whispers in the Chaos...

THE DOGWOODS ARE BLOOMING after all. Of course, I knew they would—somewhere. But I couldn't help but dread the desolation this spring was sure to unveil in our yard after last winter's icy "storm of the century."

I have always considered the dogwoods surrounding our home a special gift from God. Certainly, we had no idea they were here that snowy winter we crossed several barbed-wire fences to explore this wooded, ravine-circled property. And it was only by His grace that we didn't cut them down when we cleared it so we could build. But my loving Father knew I had always wished for a dogwood tree, and He gave me not just one, but so many we still sometimes beg people to take the saplings that grow so freely here.

There hasn't been a spring since that I haven't thanked Him with all my heart for allowing me to live in this place that is wrapped in such beauty and peace.

I even managed to thank Him for His mercies—eventually—in that dark, ice-covered December when winter's furious blast brought weeks without heat or lights or water; and we could only watch helplessly as our trees exploded like shotgun blasts and massive limbs crashed around us in great thundering showers of ice and shattered wood. Even so, didn't we give Him thanks

58

when more than one huge missile missed a window by only inches? Didn't we agree it was by God's grace that my ice-encrusted pussy willow (the one Mac had been warning was dangerously tall) did almost no damage when it fell across my little brick porch, mercifully between my sunroom windows and my fish pond? Wasn't it His intervention that its top barely brushed my garden fence? Didn't we confess how blessed we were when neighbors showed up unannounced to help clear the lane so we could get out? And didn't we finally have the presence of mind to just praise Him for His awesome creativity and enjoy the intricate beauties of my ice-laced garden?

But I couldn't help but mourn my dogwoods. Their perfect canopies—fashioned by God's own hand— were now marred by twisted, broken limbs, and my usual eagerness for spring felt twisted and broken, too.

Now, here is His marvelous paradox of love: This spring my yard overflows with life. Those broken, twisted dogwoods flaunt drifts of creamy white, with delicate, cross-shaped blossoms crowding every branch. Grape hyacinth (...for the soul...?) scatter themselves across the still-dead lawn, joyfully heralding spring's arrival. Forsythia explode in sun-kissed yellow, then drop their flowers to float on my pond like tiny golden stars. And the redbuds, not to be outdone, robe every graceful twig in royal hue.

And here is the "pressed down, running over" part: The dogwood at the bottom of the hill... the one we almost cut down because half of it is lying on the ground... the one I couldn't help but grieve every time we drove down our lane... is gloriously, defiantly covered in blooms! How the half that is still attached to the "mother tree" by only a little strip of flesh could even be alive, let alone bloom so profusely, is a mystery. It probably will have to eventually come off so the rest of the tree can recover. But for now, it sings the Creator's power and grace, and testifies to precious truths.

The God of hope always has a plan, especially when our eyes say, "hopeless," and it is always "joy unspeakable and full of glory!" Creator God loves to lavish improbable beauty in unlikely places, just because He is.

Our Redeemer is in the business of taking the most broken, twisted things in our lives and covering them with the purist, most elegant splendor. As long as we stay connected to the Source, even a tiny bit, the possibilities are astonishing.

And if we listen for His still, small voice, we will always hear His tender love whisper in the chaos.

...and Improbable Beauty in Unexpected Places

I've gardened long enough to know it is an undeniable truth. If I want my plants to flourish and produce, I must be willing to prune—sometimes unmercifully.

The white crepe myrtle at the edge of the slope seemed past saving. I really wanted some kind of blooming shrub to anchor the rustic steps leading up the hillside to our front yard. But those bushes simply did not get enough sun to bloom, and that lack of sun had made them so tall and "leggy" there was nothing left of their natural beauty. So there didn't seem much to lose when we decided to cut them down. Usually, I have to grit my teeth and remind myself that pruning is best for the plant, and ultimately, for our pleasure. But this time, our goal was to just get rid of those tall, scraggly eyesores.

I love my Father's sense of humor. I can almost see the twinkle in His eye when He has some little, unexpected gift waiting for me; and it is always wrapped in His lesson *du jour.*

Now, for the first time in years, those hillside steps are framed by graceful bushes—fresh and green and shaped the way a crepe myrtle should be shaped. Those merciless pruning shears have done their job, and with the dead wood gone, the bushes have new life.

And here is a tiny, happy paradox: the icy devastation I mourned last winter caused just the right limbs to fall. Those sun-starved bushes now are bathed in light. And if I'm faithful to prune again at the right time, next summer their fragrant white plumes will grace our hillside just when other blooms have withered.

I love my Father's sense of humor—He always gives much more than we expect—but I confess I still can't help but dread His pruning shears. I know it's for my good, and more important, for His pleasure. So here is my sacrifice of praise: The dead wood has to go, and every limb that keeps the Son from shining through must fall. And I am grateful He will faithfully, relentlessly keep pruning—even when I flinch—until I'm finally fresh and green and shaped the way a child of His should be.

Chapter 15
Pursuing Happiness & Planting Joy

THERE IS NO QUESTION about it, grief is very, very personal. And only Sovereign God knows how long that road must be for each of us.

For my mother, it was a five-year odyssey of loneliness—of leaving home and friends of twenty years to rebuild a life that always before had centered around my father. Who could have seen the pain in her heart as she walked through each day, doing all the things that make life function: turning her little house above the creek into a home, planting new gardens, renewing old friendships, singing and teaching and serving her new church family, and loving on the children who were her other lifelong passion. I certainly did not—at least, not after those first few months—until that moment we were headed home from a day of shopping for the flowers we both loved. I have no idea how I responded (I hope it was helpful, or at least appropriate) because it took me by complete surprise: "I've suddenly realized that for the first time since your dad died, I can be happy again. It's been a long five years!"

For me, that day has slipped quietly into my heart. There is no specific point when I suddenly realized I could "be happy again." Just fewer and fewer moments surprised by depression and sorrow, and more and more moments surprised by gladness.

It is such a relief when "happy" comes. I wonder how the prophet Jeremiah faced each morning, knowing there would be no "happy" in his life. I treasure little moments when my heart is light and free again. It's been a long three years.

But here's the inexorable paradox: The more that we demand—or search for—"happy," the more elusive it becomes. Like the butterflies that grace my garden, it cannot be coaxed or called.

I love it when the butterflies come, and if I'm in the right place at the right time, their bright wings and graceful ballet bring great pleasure. But they come only when and where they choose, and pleasure only briefly, from a distance. (If I tried to grasp and hold one it would die, and crumble into dust.)

I can, however, prepare a place to welcome them. I can learn which herbs and flowers nurture them, and plant their favorites in a sunny spot where they can dry their wings, and maintain little boggy places where they drink, and make sure no poisons curse their world... and praise Creator God when they come.

So, I've hauled those demands for "happy" to the compost pile and I'm cleaning up my garden to prepare a "welcome" place. And as I work and wait and praise, the Gardener comes to work with me, and shows me this most precious paradox:

Butterflies (and happiness) are only fleeting blessings, little gifts we can't deserve and never can control, even when we create the right environment and plant the right "stuff." But in the sacrifice of cleaning up and preparing... the hard work of digging and planting and watering and weeding... the anticipation of watching and waiting and trusting... great reward is sown. The work itself is privilege, and in the garden where I seek His pleasure—invested with my heart and hope and sweat and blisters—strong, sustaining <u>joy</u> will grow, and welcome little "happy's" when they come.

My mother may have always yearned for the happy feelings she enjoyed with my father, but the deep, abiding joy of walking with <u>her</u> Father sustained her and blessed others through five years of grieving her loss, and many years beyond.

I may always yearn for "happy" to light where I can touch it, and shrink from grief that comes my way. But my Gardener plans for joy that lasts forever. If I prepare a place to welcome Him, He promises He will come, and help me purge the poisons that curse my world. But as we plow and plant and water, He warns me there is darkness still to come, and then entreats me to remember that's what flowers need to grow.

So we walk here in the twilight, and I am learning to delight in His abiding love. And when the darkness falls again and I can barely hear His voice, I know He'll breathe His promise one more time: "Weeping may endure for a night, but joy comes in the morning."

And in that promise lives my story's paradox: tears in the dark bring joy in the light, and this darkness is only the shadow of my bridge.

Chapter 16
of Elephants in the Garden...

THE ELEPHANT IS BACK. We always knew it might be... someday... but good report after good report had eased our anxieties, and we have chosen (mostly successfully) to treasure each day and heed the admonition that "...love hopes all things..."

We've been seeing its tracks all summer. At first they were so faint the wind would blow them away, and we would breathe a sigh of relief and conclude they were not really there after all.

Next, it was just one or two big prints that appeared at the edge of the yard and then disappeared back into the woods.

Then, some of our most treasured flowers were trampled (and God reminded me—again—how the sweetest fragrance is released).

Eventually, they led boldly to our sunroom windows; and as beady eyes glared in, we thought surely those menacing tusks might shatter at least one. (No cute, fat cartoon character or docile circus performer this. This elephant is huge and ugly, and breathtakingly ominous.)

Now it has taken up residence just outside our door. At times it crowds everything else from our lives. It is hard to walk in the yard without sinking into the deep depressions caused by cruel feet that appear to have targeted Mac's arm while we were busy with life. And after a summer of endless tests and so many x-rays our friends are asking if he glows in the dark, we are still waiting—still unsure if there is a problem.

It is the waiting that is the hardest. How do you fight what you do not know? But it is one of God's greatest tools to shape and polish us; so it is back to the classroom again. Time to learn (again)...

...the trust that grows from praying in ever deeper ways;

...the love and encouragement of family and friends (and the privilege of giving it);

...the joy of knowing that others pray for us; and most glorious of all,

...the mind-boggling truth that Jesus prays for us!

Can you see Him there? Sitting at Almighty God's right hand... surrounded by all the glories of heaven... and thinking about us! He knows our every hurt and fear. His heart is so tender toward our need He lives to intercede for us. It is so unbelievably personal... He continually, lovingly speaks Mac's name—and mine—into the Father's ear!

Will He answer with more sweet gifts for which I never would have thought to ask—the kind you only truly can appreciate in retrospect? Absolutely. It is what He does. To be honest, right now I would gladly settle for just a mundane, "never mind—nothing there." But whatever lies ahead, His sweetest gift is this: Jesus prays for me, and He is waiting at the bridge.

...and Tales of Tails

It seems almost anti-climactic. Of course, I'm tremendously relieved and thankful that the verdict—after all this time and all those tests—is "never mind... nothing there!" I know a million little blessings came out of that time of waiting. We are trusting God a little more and accepting a little more readily His ways we don't understand.

What can we say but "Your will, Your way, Lord," when Mac finally gets a clean bill of health just as his best friend and lifelong boating-hunting-fishing buddy is dying of brain cancer only four weeks after it is discovered!

How can we not say "Praise Your name," to know that this feisty friend we loved met his Redeemer with joyful anticipation in spite of terrible pain and suffering.

How can I not be touched by the visible lightening of Mac's countenance and spirit at this reprieve, even in the midst of his grief, and not speak gratitude to see that fearsome elephant trudging slowly out of our lives!

It looks almost laughable from behind—not nearly so big as it had seemed—head hanging low, once threatening tusks dragging the ground, little scraggly tail swinging limply as it plods out of sight.

So, why is there disappointment in my gratitude? I realize it is this; there is no little gift tied to that tail. This time He has granted exactly what I asked—a mundane "never mind"—and nothing more.

Along this path of pain and paradox, He has called me to praise Him in the most unexpected places for the most unlikely things, but always with a thrill of excitement for the outcome.

This time He calls me to just plod along it—sort of like that shrinking, totally un-menacing elephant with the pitiful, pathetic tail.

This time He calls me to praise Him just because He is.

This time this path holds no new revelations... no warm, fuzzy lessons... no intriguing paradox.

This time all I hear is that He has called me to this path... that it will lead me to my bright and shining bridge... that He is waiting there for me.

And that's enough!

Chapter 17
A Riddle...

THIS ADVENTURE along the Path of Praise is the most amazing paradox! As we stand here in the middle of the road and look back, the route along which we've come is stunningly bright and clear! But didn't it often look dark and confusing as we struggled along? Didn't we sometimes feel as if the very next step would be the one that did us in? And isn't it just like our loving God that that is the very step that brings us the most joy and hope for the future!

In retrospect, we wouldn't trade those dark times for anything. I'd like to believe "the experience of my faith" has finally, irrevocably brought me to complete and immediate assurance that no matter how dark it seems, God is <u>there</u>, steadfastly working all things for our good, immutably <u>enough</u>. But here is the most wondrous, troubling, exciting paradox: That confidence of faith is only a pleasant plateau in this voyage—a place to rest and gain strength for battles yet to come. Just as the darkness of the pit was God's best tool to nurture and strengthen my faith, so the next difficult leg of the journey will be His means for completing His work in us.

The road ahead winds ever upward... still obscure... still sometimes ominous... harder than ever before... and it has taken another unexpected, inexplicable turn. While we've been celebrating Mac's complete recovery from lung cancer, his body has silently, mysteriously begun attacking itself! No one so far has been able to find what is causing his terrible skin rashes and agonizing itch. It seems worse every day, and we are finding ourselves dreading the night.

The general diagnosis is "dermatitis," but so far the source of "IT" remains a mystery. Doctors here at home and in St. Louis are not using the "C-word," but this battle is beginning to have a faint odor of "elephant." A scary thought, but I agree with Mac: If that is what it is, we would rather know it and deal with it. Whatever IT is, unless God chooses to miraculously intervene (we know He could, and would if that was His best plan for all He wants to do in our lives), we are in for a long haul.

We are disappointed at the lack of concern we encounter at Barnes Jewish Hospital in St. Louis, but at least we have an appointment at the Mayo Clinic in Jacksonville, Florida, and we are so grateful for prayer warriors who faithfully walk this path with us, petitioning for relief and rest and—finally—answers.

While we certainly long for relief and answers, we recognize this is just part of life in a fallen world. We truly want to embrace—with His unspeakable joy—the adventure we've been given. We really do want to let Him finish the work He has begun in this, His way. But He also says to ask and keep on asking and seek and keep on seeking, so we will keep on asking for complete healing and ever more trust in His goodness, and we resolve to keep on seeking His wisdom and courage when it all seems so overwhelming.

So, here at the intersection of the road already travelled and the dark and mysterious path yet to come, the refreshing fragrance of "enough" washes over us, sweetly banishing the stench of "elephant."

...wrapped in a Mystery...

Undoubtedly, the greatest blessing in this journey is our Father's presence. As we face this next big challenge, His mercy keeps us going.

By now Mac looks like a burn victim, skin as red as any boiled lobster, arms so swollen the flesh is actually splitting and weeping. Then we discover that he is just that! His body is literally burning itself up from the inside. It is called erythroderma—"red skin"—and I think it could not be more aptly named. This vital, largest-of-our-body organ that we seldom think about can no longer regulate his temperature and he is at risk of life-threatening hypothermia. If we cannot get him where he can obtain the right kind of help he will not make it through the week; but his Jacksonville Mayo appointment is still two months away, and he is in no condition to travel that far, anyway. Appeals to Mayo in Rochester to "fit us in" bring only "So sorry! If you want to come to ER, we'll be glad to treat you there." We think that is just too ambiguous to risk the ten-hour drive to Minnesota.

But bless his dermatologist's caring heart! He stays on the phone until finally we have an appointment in Rochester—day after tomorrow! Though we are elated, a five-hundred-mile drive seems daunting. At times Mac chills so hard it is frightening. Not much we can do except wrap him in blankets and try our best to keep him warm—and pray a lot, of course—until we get him where they know how to treat him.

I have learned enough along this path to appreciate how much we really do need each other. My plea for "help with skin on" goes out and we are immediately inundated with calls: "How can we help?... We're praying... What do you need?... Can we take care of 'the boys' or your gardens?... We'd be glad to drive you..." and we find ourselves on a rollercoaster of thanksgiving and hope and fear. (I never have liked rollercoasters.)

Mac is convinced we need to leave as soon as we can. We'll need to take our time on the road, and stop to rest overnight. He has gone from the hypo/hyper-thermic crisis of yesterday to being strong enough today to drive all the way to Des Moines. We know there is absolutely no explanation for that except the prayers of friends who love us, and God's Hearing Heart. (Maybe this rollercoaster is not quite so bad after all.)

After a full night's sleep in Des Moines (we truly are amazed—and grateful!), Mac is sure he feels strong enough to drive again. Thirty minutes later the rollercoaster takes another breathtaking plunge and he is barely able to pull the car to the side of the road and move to the passenger seat. As we arrive in Rochester he is in complete crisis, and I am profoundly grateful for God's timing and presence. If we had decided to wait and drive straight through we would have been somewhere along the road when he crashed...

We're relieved that six hours in ER reveal no problems with any vital organs—except that biggest, least-appreciated one, of course. But the Mayo system is just that—several institutions that function as an independently cooperative organism, and if they admit him through this hospital's ER he will miss his appointment with dermatology in the Clinic. So, armed with Valium to calm his overloaded systems, it is back to the hotel where, in spite of my trepidation, we both get another good night's sleep. (One of the blessings of this journey is the gratitude God is teaching for the little, mostly un-noticed things. I think I will never again fail to appreciate the gift of a good night's sleep!)

This morning we hope to finally begin getting some answers. Well, actually we've hoped for that at every step of this adventure, but this time, batteries of exams, tests, biopsies, scans, etc., and meetings with the dermatologist and hospitalist have brought us to the in-patient arm of the Mayo system, where surely this world-renowned medical powerhouse will find what has so far eluded less-celebrated experts.

Mac will be treated in the Rochester Methodist Hospital ICU for at least the next several days in what will probably be a pretty uncomfortable process. This man who does not sit still well, even on his best day, will be wrapped like a mummy in steroid-soaked "wet dressings" and covered with hot blankets every three hours, with only a few minutes' break in between. Our prayers are not only for this treatment to be successful and finally identify the source of his problems, but for his complete rest in God's strength during these long stretches of immobility.

And since we are here for a longer stay than we anticipated, I need to find a cheaper place to stay.

The progress is much slower than we would like, but the wet dressings and other treatments have helped. His skin is beginning to look human again, and much of the swelling is gone. However, even after four days and nights in isolation with round-the-clock treatment, rash is showing up on new areas of his body. Amazing! There was not much of him left that didn't already have it. It seems apparent that just treating symptoms is a losing battle, though they continue to do a wonderful job of that here. Our hope now is that all those tests will finally begin to identify the source of IT so we can concentrate on prevention.

I am now at a hotel right across the street from the hospital—old but cheaper, clean (mostly), and certainly convenient. My Father knows when I need a good laugh in the midst of chaos, and when I realize I have to stand in the hall to maneuver my suitcase into the closet and then barely have room to walk between the bed and dresser to step up into the tiny, old-fashioned bathroom, well...

Though I truly have never seen such a minuscule hotel room, the big bed that fills it is comfortable and inviting. I remind myself how much I like "antiques;" and once I surrender my expectations—Mac usually asks to see the room in unfamiliar venues before we commit to staying <u>anywhere</u>—I find it sort of quaint and charming. And I'm grateful for that big, almost-antique, definitely-not-flat-screen TV in the corner where I can watch endless episodes of NCIS and escape for a while when I am not at the hospital.

The struggle for rest continues. I am comforted by the aura of "sanctuary" that pervades this town dedicated to hope and healing, but severe storms with tornado warnings two nights in a row; a huge, old-fashioned window that <u>is</u> the wall by my bed; two little dogs that hate storms; and the reality that I could need to get myself and two dogs out of that room and down the stairs in a hurry result in very *un*-restful nights! (And "the boys" just cannot figure out why they have to sleep with their leashes on.) But I do love a good thunderstorm, so I revel in God's awesome reminder that it is His voice that thunders and flashes over the elegant downtown buildings I can see from that big old-fashioned window by my bed.

I'm just beginning to think the worst might be over when Mac calls to tell me they've moved everyone to shelter in the halls. It's OK, though—he's having a good time visiting with other patients and showing his nurse "how to make good coffee" in the little family lounge. I'm touched to realize how much he's missed the socializing that is such a part of who he is. And I think I may just have to accept this longing for sleep as my "new normal."

It is still a day-to-day battle. Right before this last onslaught of new rashes, they said they might let Mac go home. Now we wonder if it might be longer. Stress definitely seems to exacerbate the rashes, so my prayer requests go out again: *This prolonged stay at Mayo is not covered by any of our insurance...we need the lake lot we placed on the market a couple weeks ago to sell quickly, and Mac needs to stop feeling guilty about my "having to just sit around so much" at the hospital. (Not that I don't appreciate his concern...)*

There is no way to express how much the constant assurances of prayer and concern for us mean. Every email and call is precious. While we know we're where we need to be right now, days like yesterday can feel a long way from home, and we are grateful we still find our friends and family's love and prayers—and His love through them—every step of the way. God smiles at their faithfulness with those cups of cold water, and so do we, and we pray He'll help us be as faithful to ask for the same sweet assurance of His presence for them!

...inside an Enigma

It's good to be home, but we seem to be in a tug-of-war with IT: One day a little better; the next, struggling to hold the ground we've made; the next, not even sure how much ground we've actually made.

IT moved into Mac's ears a few days ago. We laughed that he looked like he'd just lost a boxing match, but last night was really tough. One ear is swollen nearly shut and very painful; and both eyes and the bridge of his nose are swollen. What do we do with that... wet-wrap his head?!

He is amazingly patient—doubly amazing for such a high-energy, git-er-done guy! But I know he is so sick of being miserable and finding no light at the end of the tunnel. My heart breaks as I watch him struggle with uncertainty in <u>everything</u>... Will Dr. Matlock want to continue his care since he had reached an impasse before we went to Mayo? Did we make that expensive, exhausting trip to Mayo for nothing? Has our confidence in this region's VA system been misguided? Where in the world do we go from here?

The truth is, there is only one place to go, and I dive into my Father's arms, comforted to find the prayers of our traveling companions already there; reassured by His promise that He will help us stand against Satan's efforts to discourage and defeat us.

I'm so thankful for the transparency of God's Word. He promises that our light and momentary troubles are achieving for us an eternal glory that far outweighs them all; and if the great Apostle Paul struggled with "being human" there is hope for us! I am grateful. I want to trust—with joy—what we cannot possibly understand, and in faith "...fix [my] eyes not on what is seen, but what is unseen." I truly want Him to use all of it (IT!) for His glory.

So now the verdict is in... it is back to Mayo again! By the time we had to make the final decision, it had become clear it was best to keep Mac's appointment with the internist they wanted him to see. And as always, God was one step ahead of us. He knew we would be battling to regain ground from a pretty scary flare up. Now we will not only see the internist, but the dermatologist, who rearranged his schedule to see Mac while we are there. God bless the Mayo philosophy and people who live it... and our own Dr. Matlock! Without his extraordinary effort we would not have been at Mayo in time to save Mac's life, and my heart is touched when I remember his heart-rending "...wish I could have done more..." as we left.

But we both are a little more weary each day. Ten hours on the road sounds even longer than before, and I confess I can't quite forget that frightening last few hours before we could get to ER the last time. My prayer requests now include *courage and peace* for <u>one</u> of us, and I wonder how we can ever express how much all the love, prayers, calls, emails, Facebook messages, offers of help and scripture quotes mean to us. (I love it when they write them out—they always seem to be exactly what we need at that moment.)

Did I mention I have <u>never</u> liked roller coasters? I never could see much sense in struggling up a steep hill just so the bottom could drop out from under me in the next breath. What kind of fun is that! So-o-o, this is one of those times it's a good thing we'd already made the commitment to take this adventure we've been given. We are definitely on a roller coaster of paradoxes right now.

We really, really like the internist at Mayo. We really, really <u>do not</u> like his message: "...with your history and this rash that keeps popping up, just think we need to turn over every rock. Let's make sure there are no little cells hiding somewhere. Even if there aren't, we need to keep a close watch... unexplained rashes could be a harbinger of lymphoma..." (Mac says we should be looking for <u>large</u> cells hiding somewhere since his cancer was <u>large</u> cell.) So we are in another round of tests, lab work, exams, assessments and consultations.

We really, really liked the dermatologist last time. We were so impressed with his immediate grasp of the problem after just a few moments of scanning the voluminous medical record we handed him, and he seemed willing to patiently entertain every question and concern we expressed. But this time... he was very, very busy... where did we get the lymphoma reference... the diagnosis <u>is</u> severe dermatitis and Mac <u>is</u> better... we just need to accept that in many cases like this the cause is never found, so stay with the intensive treatment regimen he prescribed and give it time... here is a brochure he should have given us that explains that...

Ultimately it is certainly a better diagnosis, but the prospect of ongoing misery and endless treatments with no real light at the end of the tunnel is pretty disappointing. Mac is ready to just get in the car and come home; but thankfully the rollercoaster hits a level spot and we catch our breath and begin working on "we've expected too much—even Mayo can't have all the answers—let's play this hand out."

And so we pray (again) for :

...extra mercy and grace as we work to accept His "no."

...His perfect plan in our lives, and our trust and obedience in all this.

...Extra courage and endurance—and submission—as we contemplate: wet wraps (Mac hates them and they wear me out); creams and ointments (ick); sleepless, itchy, miserable nights; dread of another scary flare with no understanding of why or how to avoid it; and no discernible end in sight.

We are headed home again this morning, finally! "The boys" are ready! They're good little travelers, but they are so tired of being cooped up in hotel rooms or confined to a leash—it is so their nature to run, and run, and run... Usually after their morning walk they snuggle back in bed a while, but we had to laugh this morning when instead, they stationed themselves at the door and waited.

Two weeks ago we made this trip with some disappointment that there was still no answer for Mac's misery; much hope that the next battery of tests, doctors, and Mayo expertise would solve the mystery; and great appreciation for all the prayers and God's promise that He hears and answers. Those prayers, and ours, have not been in vain. He has heard and answered. But "no" is a hard answer to hear, and frankly, neither of us like it! (Might as well confess it—He knows our hearts.)

We do know He definitely has a purpose in this, that it is very possible we may never know exactly what that purpose is in this life, and through the experience of our faith, that trusting Him along a dark path brings the greatest blessings of all. But only He knows how many times I've prayed, along with that father of the demon-possessed boy, "Lord, I believe..."

We try to find comfort in knowing that Mayo's research arm might someday use Mac's situation to help others (we signed up), and we truly are grateful that this last, intensive battery of tests showed absolutely no errant cancer cells or other underlying problems anywhere. Truly.

We truly appreciate Dr. Liggett's concern that these rashes could be "a very early warning shot across the bow" that we need to watch, and that he will be there for us if he is ever proven right. Truly.

And we truly know that in the grand scheme of things, things could be much worse. Truly. You cannot walk the halls of the vast Mayo Complex without being convicted of that. But even though the man with no shoes pities the man with no feet and understands his situation could be worse, his feet still hurt when they are cold. So-o-o, we probably need those prayers more than ever while we adjust to "no shoes" status. It is probably not going to change any time soon.

We're disappointed Mac isn't well enough to do the sightseeing we planned before we leave Rochester—it seems like such a gracious town—but our merciful Redeemer reminds us as we head back home that He has already more than made up for it as we drove up:

The zero-visibility, "toad-strangler" thunderstorm we ran into just a few miles before we reached Kansas City brought both "boys" out of their little beds in the back seat and into my lap in one leap, then just stopped as we got to the outskirts of the city.

The GPS-boggling road construction in the city went from frustrating to funny when "Molly" kept routing us right back into it. We decided it is definitely time to get her little brain updated, and about the third time around agreed that sometimes the ones God gave us actually work much better.

The thunderstorms on the other side of Kansas City were awesome to watch as our route ran right between them. We reveled in amazingly brilliant blue skies bracketed by towering thunderheads and flashes of lightning, and then marveled at the stunning rainbow that suddenly spanned the breach. We knew it was another sweet gift from God, and we watched it for miles. I have never seen one so defined—standing on a dazzling, fat base one could see all the way to the ground. It seemed like a double blessing that this one had its own shadow—

just a hint of a twin beside it—and God reminded me that unanticipated rainbows are my Father's promise and love revealed.

Though we leave without the answers for which we long, the elegant comfort and patient/visitor friendliness of the Mayo system is still a blessing. They really do make the whole experience so much easier, and never challenge—in fact, welcome—the need for family members to be involved at every step of the way. And we know it is no coincidence that the dermatologist referred us to this particular internist, who we find has walked this path before Mac. He tells us he had a mystifying rash all over his face for years before he finally was diagnosed with lymphoma—even with all his Mayo resources! He is still in treatment, but after four years of being unable to work, is back and acts and looks great. It explains a little his urgency that we not take anything for granted. While Mac is still working through all we heard, we know whatever IT is, it is what it is, and we are finding it curiously comforting that this renowned physician is so unafraid to "speak the truth in love," and so willing to "turn over rocks..."

And one more sustaining truth: Though this has unquestionably been the hardest five years of our lives, without it we would never have known the privilege of "the fellowship of His suffering" ...or the tender mercies of His demanding discipline... or the sweetness of walking one step at a time, learning to trust Him more with each step. And we would never have known so intimately what a wonderful thing His family really is. We are truly grateful.

We still hope someday to find out *"why."* It would be a relief to know how to avoid and prevent, and we will keep exploring all avenues that open to us. Our constant prayer is that in God's time the real problem will be found, but more important that we will keep praising our patient Teacher, Who not only puts up with all our *"why's,"* but ever so gently uses them to teach us His goodness and sovereignty. We are humbled by how sweetly He keeps drawing us closer and closer to Him through every little skirmish we would avoid if we could, but now wouldn't trade for a million dollars. We pray that same sweet playing out of His plan in every life—especially those we love. There is nothing more precious, nor awe-filled, than to fall into the hand of the Living God!

Chapter 18
Finding Hope...

THIS MOUNTAIN ROAD is always beautiful and—unlike the path of praise to which we are called—ever inviting.

I especially love it in spring, when evergreen pine and cedar brighten still-dormant oak and hickory forests and wild cherry blossoms begin to scatter themselves through the woodland. Each day brings new life, and as the fruit flowers fade a few green leaves emerge and drifts of white serviceberry blooms appear, beckoning the redbuds to follow. And not long after, dogwoods cloak hillside and ravine as uncounted hues of green unfold.

Summer brings lavish green branches that over-arch whole sections of the road. Sun pierces through the shade in bright shafts that dance ahead, summoning us to "come further in and further up." Wildflowers adorn ditches and slopes in an ever-changing kaleidoscope of color and texture; and we drive a little slower, vigilant for deer or foxes or low-flying owls that suddenly appear out of nowhere; admiring wild turkey and quail that explode in clouds of feathers as we pass; hoping for one more glimpse of the cougar that calmly shepherded her cub across the road in front of us a few years ago.

Fog and mist often shroud early morning drives, rendering these mountain lanes magical and other-worldly; and rainy days here seem somehow friendly and invigorating as towering clouds thunder and flash through the trees.

There was a time when these steeply winding roads were flint rock and gravel; a notoriously *un*-friendly route known as "That Road!!" that inflicted at least one flat tire on any who dared venture here. It was always a relief to reach the last two level miles leading to our lake house—providing one could make it through the quarter mile of bottomless mud in the middle. The way is friendlier now—thirteen miles of well-maintained blacktop or chip-and-seal—guarded by forest and cliff and Goat Hill Farm and Buck James' sleek chocolate-and-cream ponies.

By fall the hillsides are a riot of color, uncounted shades of green turning orange and gold and red and yellow and russet, more than worth the hundred-mile drive to admire. We scramble to schedule just the right weekend for our annual boat tour, calculating the date the foliage will be at its best. We pray for sunshine and calm winds and good health for all who plan to come, then gather to convoy down the lake to the campground *du jour* where we will stop to grill hamburgers and fry potatoes ("here's the one with <u>no onions</u>, Mac!") and set out whatever side dishes these boaters decide to bring this year. It is a great way to renew old friendships and make new ones, and the memories are, as the old commercial goes, priceless!

Winter brings its own beauty. Mac always laments the "ugliness" of Missouri in the winter, but I don't see it that way. I marvel at the spectacular lake vistas one sees from every high point, mostly obscured by forest the rest of the year. One realtor described it as a "seasonal lake view." We laughed at that. I'm not sure I would want a house where one could only see the lake "seasonally" (aka winter) but those "seasonal lake views" make a winter drive along these Mark Twain Forest byways a breathtaking journey, day or night. And when it snows... well... the word "fairyland" is no exaggeration, though I would just as soon enjoy it from the safety of my deck. Snow and icy patches on those mountain roads make the adventure just a little too breathtaking for my liking.

This spring evening, ninety-year-old Earl, long-time neighbor and World War II vet, occupies the front passenger seat of Mac's Dodge Ram on a jaunt to Kimberling City, not far from Branson. We will meet his younger brother—also a World War II vet but "only" eight-one—and other lake neighbors at The Filling Station on Highway 13, halfway there.

The little restaurant lives up to its "famous fried chicken" boast, and as we leave, our table is quickly claimed by the large group waiting at the door. Now it is on to the bi-weekly Blue-Grass Concert-on-the-Parking-Lot at the shopping center overlooking the graceful steel arches of the Kimberling City Bridge.

Triangle flags of red-white-and-blue festoon the rope barrier marking off the seating area in front of The Hillbilly Bowl and Restaurant. (Bring your own lawn chairs, of course.) The stage is an old flatbed truck, its cab's side panels emblazoned with "Missouri Boat Ride" and fortified with all the necessary sound and lighting and, of course, "Old Glory" waving in the evening breeze.

The band is a regional favorite, boasting one of the famous "Darling Brothers" from the old "Mayberry RFD" TV show, and the lead singer performs with special distinction tonight: his "pickin' hand" is still swollen and painful from a copperhead snake bite a couple days before.

In addition to their own show, The Missouri Boat Ride Blue Grass Band uses this venue to promote incredibly talented young blue-grass groups—often entire families or ensembles of teens and pre-teens from surprising addresses like Flagstaff, Arizona, and Athens (pronounced $\bar{A}$-thens), Illinois—who exuberantly regale us with songs of devotion for country and family, and unabashedly speak the name of Jesus with love and reverence. Impromptu fund-raisers are often added to the docket, and tonight the crowd responds to the need of a former band member awaiting a kidney transplant with donations of nearly $5,000.

It will be hard to say goodbye to all that this represents. The lake house we built with our own hands, one section at a time over a ten-year period... where five generations of the Mac Clan celebrated holidays and vacations and found refuge from the stresses of life (and offered it to others)... and entertained all the kids' best friends and played cousins card games till two in the morning... and learned to run trot lines and water ski and drive the boat and perfect water skills and cliff dive... and suffered injuries and sunburns and near-disasters and exciting trips to the ER... has been sold! It is a necessary thing. "IT" has taken its toll, and maintenance and care for two homes a hundred miles apart has become more burden than joy; but the thought of leaving it behind still brings tears. I don't doubt it is the right thing to do at the right time—Mr. Mac's wise financial management has given us a better-than-deserved lifestyle for years—and after all, it really is just stuff. We yearn to be His children of Light and bless those with whom we are dealing, and honor Him in all we do and say. But still...

It is really, really hard!

...Believing a Future

"I know this has been the hardest few years of our lives, but I think it's been the best!"

I've known that, too, but hearing it from this man who spent those years suffering, overcoming one crisis only to be inundated by the next, is truly awe-inspiring. And the fact that it is now spoken from a wheelchair... well...

We are pretty sure the wheelchair thing is only temporary. As soon as they figure out whether it is his back or hip or something else causing this intense pain—and then figure out how to fix it—he will be on his feet again. But in the meantime, it means another round of doctor's appointments and tests and x-rays; even more battles with IT (stress and pain seem to always kick it into high gear); and worst of all, diminished mobility and increased dependence on others—the hardest challenge of all for a macho, jeans-and-flannel-shirt kind of guy!

And though we try to ignore it, there is always that faint stench of "elephant" in the midst of it all...

It is not true "you can't teach an old dog new tricks" when the Master Teacher is in the classroom. I am so grateful—and enormously humbled—that He never gives up... even when the "Jack Russell" in us still requires "the short leash"... even after we have learned its lessons time and again. I can't help but wonder how we would be dealing with this latest "hurry up and wait" crisis if it were not for those lessons. If experience is the best teacher, then the experience of our faith is indisputably the ultimate educator. And we celebrate that, if not for that bout with the wheelchair, Mac would have missed a special day with daughter Kim, zooming through the mall Christmas shopping, laughing and lunching and making memories, just the two of them.

God is faithful. His promise of hope and a future never fails. And, sweet paradox, this path somehow seems easier as each step grows harder.

...Trusting His Plan

This paradox is routine by now:

Unlike that "pretty-on-the-outside, ugly-on-the-inside" hotel of the past, the downtown Little Rock hotel and convention center where we are staying is pleasant and inviting. In this comfortable room, wood and warm colors and big windows have supplanted the worn dinginess of that ugly, depressing suite of the past.

The VA hospital is being renovated. Bright colors and padded chairs inhabit waiting rooms that once were "decorated" in stark white and hard plastic.

The quiet, elegant little restaurant where the elephant first found us is gone—demolished to make room for never-ending road construction at the intersection of Inter-States 430 and 630, now a beehive of dump trucks and track loaders and men in neon green vests.

This bar and grill in downtown Little Rock is noisy and boisterous, but also elegant in a wood-paneled, old-world pub sort of way. The "business crowd" is wrapping up earnest conversation and one last drink as we find a table in a back corner, and as they trickle out, the "young crowd" arrives, manifestly determined to "have a good time." Background music blares and multiple TV's offer various sports broadcasts at ever-increasing volume, though no one seems to notice. Then the "convention crowd" descends. Middle-aged, overweight men and women talk too loudly and laugh too stridently and seem to have no concern for those around them, and we wish they would at least take off the name badges proclaiming attendance at their church's convention. But we are gratified by rustic wooden plaques on the walls extolling all thing American; the food is good, the service is exceptional; and best of all, we know the elephant lies crushed under the "wheels of progress" at that convergence of highways where he first appeared.

This time the surgery is not—at least, should not be—life threatening. All the tests and exams and experts report no little cells—or large ones—lurking anywhere. (Take that, elephant!) This repair of worn vertebrae that are causing such pain and dis-function will be, amazingly, a "simple" outpatient procedure. We should be released to leave Little Rock for home the same day, or the next morning at the latest. (We've opted to stay over one more night anyway—six hours is a long ride, even when one feels well, and frequent stops for Mac to stretch and move around will be needed.)

The prospects for successful surgery are very good. It seems that every few days someone assures us this very procedure changed their life... that now they can run marathons... or haul wood... or...

I wish I could honestly say I face this next leg of the journey with excitement for what my Father plans in it. I've walked this path long enough now to know it will ultimately bring "joy unspeakable." I'm profoundly grateful that the way now feels solid and unshakable, and my heart praises the One Who always makes straight our path, even when it is still dark and dreary.

But my human spirit confesses it all seems too *deja vu.* Cheery hospital waiting rooms with comfortable padded chairs are better than bleak rooms with cheerless plastic ones, but they are still rooms filled with tired, anxious humanity—and I <u>are</u> one again. Efficient pre-op rooms and caring recovery rooms and helpful, friendly medical staff bring great reassurance, but one still wrestles with a sense of helplessness in the face of the unknown. Kindly doctors reporting, "It went well—you can see him soon" are blessing beyond measure, but we still face pain management and the challenges of recuperation and concerns about how this latest assault on his body will impact IT.

Will the anesthesia and antibiotics and after-effects surgery always brings throw him into another downward spiral just when the roller coaster seems to have slowed? Though progress is still inch by inch, we have been seeing less rash and quicker remission when it occurs. Could it be all that "voo-doo stuff," as Mac calls it, is actually working? It seems likely. His skin has not looked this normal in years! Is this the one that will last? Could this finally be the restoration for which we long? Only time will tell. But we know without any doubt the true source of his healing is our Sovereign Redeemer's mercy, and He <u>is</u> completing what He began in us.

My battle-weary spirit still wishes for more. My patient Teacher knows I still long for exciting new revelations and mysterious adventures with breathtaking conclusions. I still look for that "aha moment" in the middle of the night; some amazing twin rainbow between dark, towering clouds.

He gives us instead a humdrum, gray cloud; a slow, just-do-the-next-thing trek through the wilderness. He knows my every thought, so I confess—to Him and to our prayer warrior friends—that we are both just <u>tired</u>. My heart hears echoes of "how long, Lord," and I know it is definitely time (again) for an earnest "Your will, not mine, Sovereign God!" I'm so grateful (again) that He loves us enough to supply what we lack—especially the will to choose.

And (again) there are always little treasures hidden along the slowest, dreariest trek. Here are some with which He blesses us this time:

The very pleasant, middle-aged black man who shuttles us to that noisy, elegant pub is a study in paradoxes: a college-graduate, retired-military, family man who loves the Lord, he is more than satisfied to drive a shuttle because he has "seen it all" and "really enjoys" serving the hotel's guests and showing them his city.

The young man named Josh who transports us to another, quieter restaurant welcomes Mac's friendly chatter and we wonder how often his passengers fail to treat him with courtesy. He and Mac have gotten acquainted when he drove Mac to the hospital for his pre-op procedures, and now he gratefully shares his concern for the violence in his city and the degeneration of our country and his admiration for quarterback Tim Tebow's values and integrity. We encourage him to stay true to his own, and promise to pray for him as he "God blesses" us and drops us off at the restaurant he recommends.

The woman with whom I share one of the few electrical outlets in the surgery waiting room is excited that her husband has recently met the son he just found out he has—and celebrates the grandchildren she never thought she would enjoy. We talk of families and faith and the Joplin tornado, and she orders <u>Butterflies at the Window</u> for the Kindle I urged her to charge at "my" power outlet.

The pretty young driver with the long blond ponytail who shuttles me back and forth between hospital and hotel confides her disappointment in the selfishness and discourtesy of the church convention attenders filling our hotel, as well as the self-absorption and immorality of her own generation. She resolutely proclaims her determination to be different, to live by her parents' principles, to wait for "the right one." And then, with a twinkle adds that actually, "The Right One" has already brought her "the right one" and ""he was worth the wait!" I am touched when, as I later load the car to leave, she rushes out to tell me goodbye. I wish her well, and tell her I will pray for her.

I am grateful when the very pregnant young nurse I stop for help in finding Mac's room cheerfully delays her trip home. Though color-coded arrows on traffic-way floors are helpful, the hospital is still a huge, sprawling complex and we notice we are not the only ones needing to stop whomever we can find with a name lanyard for directions. The hospital is so full they were forced to keep Mac in recovery, where I can't stay, until evening; and when I return, I discover I need a ward number in *addition to the floor and bed number to find his room. Administrative offices are closed, and my rescuer is not sure where the neurology floor is, but she finds a doctor in his office and secures the directions we need, then escorts me all the way to Mac's room. I promise to pray for her new baby as she gives me a quick hug and smiles her way back to the elevator.*

Mac has already taken a short walk when I arrive. We celebrate the feeling already restored to his feet, and as soon as he finishes the dinner they have just delivered, ("Ya like squash, Earl? Give my roommate Earl my squash, San...") he is eager to walk again. He makes it halfway around the square before he is forced to admit he is tired. His smiling, red-haired nurse pronounces him "amazing," and thinks surely they will release him in the morning.

The drive home is a scenic sentimental journey. Who knows how many trips we made through these rolling green Boston Mountains in the twenty years my parents lived in Louisiana; but although the mountains are timeless, this route, like our Ozark Mountain road, has changed. It, too, is a much friendlier route than before. The curves are gentler and wider. Steep hills are leveled out by great sweeping bridges that span the valleys and tunnels like the Bobby Hopper near Bentonville.

Between the short dozes residual anesthesia and post-op fatigue impose on Mac, we reminisce about those always-beautiful, sometimes perilous drives, when Highway 71 would suddenly be reduced to one lane by the disappearance of part of the road. It was not at all uncommon for the outside lane of the pavement to, without warning, simply slide down the hillside.

Miraculously, we never heard that anyone had perished in any of those landslides, and by the time we made the return trip, the missing lane would somehow have been restored. (I wonder if the speed with which it was rebuilt ever contributed to the short lifespan of the pavement...)

We took a drive along that old highway, now called the Scenic Loop, a few years ago. We both wished we hadn't. Though most of the old, familiar landmarks are still there, many stand empty and abandoned, unable to survive on the few tourists who choose that route now. Highway 71 was once, for this family, a vibrant road of joy and anticipation; welcoming excited children who could not wait to see Bammie and Granddad again and their parents who loved the mountain scenery; entertaining countless "How long till we get there's?" and "I'm huuunngry's!" and warning innumerable "Don't make me stop this car's!" Now it seemed bleak and shabby, almost deserted in places, and we were reminded once again how temporary <u>everything</u> in this life really is— how truly precious is Sovereign God's promise of "hope and a future."

This time we stay on the newer, more comfortable route. And as Mac sleeps and I drive, I contemplate the bridges...

Among my many illogical fears is a pretty bad case of acrophobia. When I was just a little girl I discovered that if I walked too close to the edge of the bridge, my head would spin and my stomach feel queasy; so great soaring heights have never been my favorite place to be. I usually find myself holding my breath until we are safely on the other side.

So why this longing for my bright and shining bridge? Why do I look with such anticipation to standing at the very pinnacle, certain I'll enjoy the view? I know it is this: My Jesus is waiting there, and Perfect Love casts out fear!

There are still miles to go on this latest adventure. The restored feeling we celebrated in Mac's feet has now evolved to soreness in his back and legs, and we pray that our post-op visit will reveal no new problems. The dermatitis flare we feared has been, so far, only a few faint patches of rash here and there, easily fended off with the topical treatments he has used for years and the herbal supplements that are now a part of his regimen. He is finally a believer. The "voo doo" stuff he hates waits in the fridge each day until he chooses to drink it; but now he chooses, without my urging.

We are grateful that, at least at this point, it appears his recovery will be uneventful and he truly will soon be able to do things he has been unable to the past year or so. He is ready, and so am I...

...and Seeking His Face

He'd been talking about selling the lake house for a year or so, but none of us thought he would actually do it! Before there were more than a handful of houses on the peninsula... before we ever cleared the land... we camped there, borrowing water from a neighbor down the road. Then we set our pickup camper on the steep hillside (how did we ever <u>do</u> that!) and boated and swam and invited friends over for blackberry cobbler. (One could pick a cooler full of them in an hour or so at the old abandoned homestead at the end of the point—huge timber berries that vined into the trees and hung over our heads.) Later, we moved the camper out (how did we ever do <u>that</u>!) and replaced it with a little one-room A-frame Mac built at home and trucked down, one component at a time. Finally, we cleared the lot and built the house, adding rooms as our family grew until, just a couple years ago, Mac partitioned off the original two-bedroom open loft because, he said, our pre-teen granddaughters needed more privacy.

Its rambling cedar walls housed over thirty years of memories. Its huge deck overlooking the water welcomed planning retreats and church groups and families needing a place to get away. More friends than we can remember came to spend a night or two and play in the water. Five generations of the Mac Clan—and their friends—loved fishing and skiing and boating and swimming there. Conversations around the dining table were long and leisurely and cousins' card games included all who would play. Grandsons learned the hard way that barbed wire fences and razor-sharp flint rock were unforgiving to unprotected flesh. Friends became "family," and neighborhood "fish fry's" became a mandatory part of life on the lake.

But most of all, it was Mac's haven and sanctuary in times of crisis. Lung cancer and too many surgeries and agonizing dermatitis and the sudden death of his best friend were somehow eased by long evenings on the deck and quiet sunsets over the water and fishing with his best lake buddy. We worry that once it is gone he will long for the solace it has given him. I am reluctant—it feels like another death in the family—but he is convinced we must do this, and I've seen the wisdom of his decisions for our lives, so we sign the papers.

We are surprised at how quickly it sells; and how many times over we could have sold it. And I am surprised at the emotional toll relinquishing it continues to take on me. It really is *just stuff*—in light of eternity only a little thing—but saying goodbye feels like the final loss; and having to move in the middle of this long, intense summer the last small step toward "overwhelmed."

It truly is mostly about *just stuff*. We are not facing cancer, or the loss of a loved one, or a million other tragedies with which people we love are dealing.

But as Song of Songs 2:15 says, it is "the little foxes that ruin the vineyards." A more contemporary wise man put it this way: "We can handle the big crises. It is the little things that happen, one after another, that wear us down."

That pretty well describes it. *Little things*, one after another, have dominated our lives and worn us down.

Unquestionably the lake place is *just stuff*. Getting it ready for new owners and moving what *stuff* we choose to keep is complicated by Mac's recent surgery, but his obvious relief at being free of it convinces me it was time, and as we hand over the keys to a very excited family, I try to comfort myself that they will love it almost as much as we have.

It is all *just stuff*, but *little things* like the cedar dresser my grandfather built for me and the cradle we built for our grandson and family mementoes that have accumulated over thirty years cannot be left behind.

Our plan to unload and unpack and figure out where to put four trailer-loads of *stuff* a little at a time would have worked—if we had not come home to a house infested with fleas! The two weeks it was closed up while we were at the lake house allowed them to multiply exponentially and they just will not be defeated, even after several visits from the exterminator and daily vacuuming— of everything! We try to rationalize it is merely the price one pays for two little white dogs that bring us such joy. *Just a little thing...*

Venomous red wasps are part of life in the country. *Just a little thing*, but they are exceptionally aggressive this year. They swarm at every entrance and seem as impervious to the usual pesticides as the fleas. When one (or maybe two) manage to get under my shirt and on my leg as we move stuff into the garage, their stings leave huge, painful, angry welts that keep me awake all night in spite of Benadryl and cold compresses. And exhaustion begins to multiply—again—like the fleas.

In the grand scheme of things, a tree is *just a little thing*, but that huge, elegant tree was here long before our grandparents settled in this area. It is my favorite... the centerpiece of my shade garden... the "curb appeal" of our "back-door-friends-are-best" entry. (Note to self... never build another house where people are led to enter through the utility room!)

It was not always my favorite. For years, it had dominated an embarrassingly ugly entry. Its huge, spreading branches created such dense shade that, though we tried every grass imaginable, nothing would grow there. Finally, my daughter's enchanting shade garden inspired me, and after years of trial and error and searching for just the right plants, it has become the one part of my yard with which I am completely satisfied. I love its quiet, inviting coolness.

Now, with a flash of lightning, I am starting all over again!

We knew it had struck very close. The boom shook the house at the same time the flash blinded us, even though we were sound asleep. A thorough search affirmed there was no fire, and after Mac reset a few breakers that had been tripped, we decided we could check everything else out tomorrow after church.

It seemed strange that my car was so dirty—it had been sitting there in the garage the whole time we were at the lake—until I glanced at the window beside the car. It was shattered! Ground-up leaves and debris covered the garage (and my car). And just a few feet from the window, my beautiful white oak tree stood stripped of its bark almost all the way around its five-foot circumference.

It looked like a bomb had hit. Bark hung in huge strips or lay in equally huge chunks all over the garden and walk, from the drive on one side to the patio on the other, a space of at least seventy-five feet. Spears of bark and wood were embedded in the flower beds. Whimsical little garden gnomes that decorated the rock garden that surrounded it were in pieces, thrown yards from the tree in every direction. A decorative outdoor clock that hung on the tree was shattered by the force of the strike, parts of it thrown across the drive. The path of that deadly bolt could be easily traced, beginning sixty or seventy feet above us at the top of the tree and traveling all the way down to gouge a furrow in the ground, throwing aside like child's toys the huge rocks embedded around it. Pieces of leaves and twigs and debris were plastered to the roof and side of the house.

It is clear that if it had not been there to take the hit, the lightning would have struck directly in the middle of the garage roof and almost certainly would have caused a fire; but I confess I could not help but lament at least once (or more), "Why <u>this</u> tree, when there are so many we would not have missed at all."

There was no question it would have to come down. With the damage it had sustained, it would undoubtedly be dead within a week or two, but it would require an expert tree service to take it out of the middle of all the plants and shrubs around it without ruining everything that was left; and it was just too close to the house to risk anything less.

So we watched as professional tree removers placed their huge bucket truck and track loader right in the middle of that small garden and methodically stripped a sixty-foot-tall tree of its huge limbs, one at a time, carefully dropping them where they would do no harm. Then, the precision with which they felled the huge log that was left was amazing. Not one branch of surrounding shrubs and trees was damaged.

It is all *just stuff,* but dealing with insurance claims and repair or replacement of all that was lost from such a monster strike is wearisome at best. Who knows how lightning that strikes a tree <u>beside</u> the house can destroy so much <u>inside</u> the house! Or why the brand new replacement TV requires two visits from a repair service. Or why garage door openers keep malfunctioning even after three visits from the repairman. It is all *just stuff,* but we are grateful the new heat pump is working; and the new cooking range is ordered; and the insurance adjuster has been gracious and helpful.

It is *just a little thing.* It could have been so much worse! But now my shade garden is no more. It sits stripped of its beauty; plants that must have shade to survive wilting in the hot August sun, huge flat stump dominating the space, awaiting the rakes and shovels and TLC it will take to clean up all the debris and begin replacing plants that are lost. Soon, crisp fall mornings will defeat the oppressive heat and I must begin planning and shopping and planting new, sun-lover *stuff.* But for now my heart still hurts when I walk through that bombed-out area, and Exhaustion walks with me.

It is all *little things.* Nothing, compared to the pain and sorrow of our daughter's abusive marriage and nasty divorce. We are proud of her strength and courage and faith through it all. We say "bravo" to our grandson's determination not to hate his father and grandmother in spite of the most vindictive of attacks; and we sympathize with his younger brother, who just wants his family to be fixed. But human hearts consumed with hate and threats against our lives from those to whom we have offered only kindness are a shock. Requests for orders of protection that go on and on and a legal system that seems not to care much about "right or wrong" are a new and unwelcome part of our world.

And we are hearing that surgery may be once again on Mac's horizon. This time they find a shadow between discs in his neck, and we cannot help but think "elephant"...

God is the God of order and beauty, and He created us to long for it in our lives. Our "little foxes" have brought with them threats of harm and plagues of wasps and fleas and disorder and confusion. I know it is all *just little things*, but our lives are in chaos and my reserves are gone and now Depression shouts my name.

And so, at 4:00 a.m. on a Saturday morning, I find myself kneeling on the utility room floor sobbing "I'm so sorry!" to two little guys who stare at me in misery. They cannot understand why we are not relieving their suffering. Those unrelenting, uncontrollable fleas have set up a chain reaction of torment. In spite of our best efforts, "the boys" both scratch and lick and chew incessantly until there are hot spots and raw, red patches that nothing can relieve; and we all find it impossible to sleep. (It seems an especially bitter irony that it comes just when we are finally free from the sleeplessness Mac's skin problems brought for so long!) In desperation I rise to bathe them—again. It only makes them worse, as does everything else we try, and I am overwhelmed.

It seems that Satan's "little foxes" have won, and in the darkest hour of night I voice again the cry I thought lay far behind me on this journey: *God, where are you? God, if You love me, then why?*

It is frustrating and disappointing and... embarrassing. I have seen that shining bridge! I know my King's great truth. Nothing can touch us that is not first sifted through His fingers, for our good. It is an awe-filled, wonder-filled thing to fall into the hand of the Living God. We should welcome every challenge that makes us stronger. They will, if we allow it. This depression and exhaustion from which I suffer should be lying crushed along this path of praise.

I long to feel His tender hand and hear His gentle voice. Instead I hear only the echo of His terrible truth: If I want to find His hand, I must first and only seek His face! And so my "windy cave" is now a cold brick floor, where all is lost and only purest praise is left. It is privilege undeserved. It promises victory unimaginable. It will be joy unspeakable. But for now it must be unconditional worship, offered out of a "ruined life," where nothing but praise for His glorious grace matters.

So our journey will continue. For now we slog through the vineyard where the little foxes play, and resolve to trust the time will come when we can again enjoy watching their antics. The path will still take unexpected, sometimes disturbing turns. There will be other dark nights and—hopefully—a few more shining rainbows. Another elephant may be just around the bend, though we pray for a season to catch our breath and walk in the garden and restore our strength.

In this fallen world, pain and disappointment are undeniably a part of every life and the road will often be harder than we think it should be. We will still occasionally stumble through the dark and wish for the light... still struggle to accept His "no" and trust His absence... still long for hope to be renewed.

But here is the sweetest paradox: Just when we think we stand at the edge of the cliff and can go no further, lightning strikes (literally!) and He lovingly pushes us one more step, right into His arms! And if we offer Him all we have—even only a feeble desire to want His will—He will honor it as our sacrifice of praise and bless us with His smile.

This is His sweetest plan: He _is_ using every pain and paradox of our lives to lead us along our path of praise, and He lovingly (with a twinkle in His eye, I think) chooses the most unlikely guides for our journey.

Here is His sweetest promise: His love <u>will</u> finally bring us to our bright and shining bridge of His presence and sufficiency, and we will see His face!

And now we hear His sweetest truth: Our future is secure. Our hope is fulfilled. He waits at the pinnacle for us. And nothing is ever wasted in His economy. Even fleas. Especially pain!

ABOUT THE AUTHOR

Sandi McReynolds lives near Joplin, MO, with her husband, Mac, and "The Boys," Spanky and Scooter. The McReynolds' are active members of College Heights Christian Church, Joplin, where she serves on the Women in Ministry Board and leads Salt & Light Ministry, dedicated to informing and educating Christians about social and political issues affecting church and family.

10009297R00068

Made in the USA
San Bernardino, CA
03 April 2014